Ecumenopolis
U. S. A.

Ecumenopolis U.S.A.

THE CHURCH
IN MISSION
IN COMMUNITY

H. CONRAD HOYER

AUGSBURG PUBLISHING HOUSE
MINNEAPOLIS, MINNESOTA

ECUMENOPOLIS U.S.A.

The Church in Mission in Community

Copyright © 1971 Augsburg Publishing House

Library of Congress Catalog Card No. 74-158997

International Standard Book No. 0-8066-1120-0

MANUFACTURED IN THE UNITED STATES OF AMERICA

Contents

Foreword

No one needs to announce the fact that change is the order of the day for all the institutions of our society—including the churches. Two important factors affecting the churches are the increasing urgency of ecumenical action and the profound changes wrought by the move from the small geographic community within which the churches developed in this country to the new forms of community within which churches—and church people—must live and serve today.

This book analyzes these two factors theologically, sociologically, and in very practical terms. Each chapter emphasizes one of these aspects—the first and second laying the biblical and theological basis for unity and mission; the third moving into a sociological look at the community, yet with a distinct theological point of view. Chapter 4 summarizes in a succinct and helpful way the data on changes in the USA relating to population, mobility, affluence, the knowledge explosion, and other phenomena of our day as these affect the churches. Chapters 5, 6, and 7 are detailed expositions of three essentials for the churches if they are to cope with the present day. From his long and wide experience, Dr. Hoyer knows that the typical "muddling through" stance can result in disaster for the institutional church. Business, government, and education have learned that survival and effectiveness in a complex society require careful planning, competent administration, and an honest evaluation of every effort undertaken. Few churches and church-related organizations have as yet taken these disciplines seriously.

This is no popular, simple exhortation to do better. It is a serious, detailed presentation of facts and procedures. The reader will not skim through it casually. Rather, it may well become a tool for ministers, church executives, lay boards and committees—a tool which will be kept at hand, consulted frequently, and used as a guide for action. Perhaps no one will agree with all of it. But everyone who cares about the effectiveness of the church's mission to our troubled world will be able to learn from it. It is a book which many of us have needed for a long time.

CYNTHIA C. WEDEL

Preface

Where does the church fit in the modern world? Or does it? Thoughtful people ask, and the answers are by no means clear.

This book does not presume to give answers. Rather, it is written in hope that it will contribute to the process of finding answers and encourage readers to join in the quest for answers. The analysis and suggestions are intended to provide a constructive framework for that process.

The Author

This book summarizes insights and understandings based on my experience as a life-long member of the church of Jesus Christ, with most of that time spent in the employed service of the church. For seven years I served as a parish pastor in two Lutheran congregations. For the past 28 years, I have been in national church administration. I was the first executive secretary of the Division of American Missions of the National Lutheran Council, and served for seventeen years in that position. In 1960, I joined the staff of the National Council of Churches as Associate Director of the Division of Home Missions, and I have been Associate Director of the National Council's Commission on Regional and Local Ecumenism, or its predecessor, the De-

partment for Councils of Churches, since 1965. During
these years in national administration I have traveled
more than a million miles for the church. I have been
in every one of the fifty states, in every major metropolitan area, and in hundreds of smaller communities,
and have been related to mission strategy studies cov-
ering a wide range of concerns.

The Readers

These pages are addressed primarily to the lay people of the church. They are the people who are disturbed
by the question of the church's place in the modern
world, and they have been least helped by much that
has been said. By reflecting on these questions they can
contribute significantly to the process of discovering
answers as they serve Christ's church through their vocational pursuits, as well as through their participation
on boards and committees of congregations, ecumenical
structures, and denominations. This focus on the laity
explains the style and the approach.

Three other reader audiences loom in the background,
and perhaps they have influenced my approach and the
contents more than I know. One of my concerns is for
the young seminary graduate as he moves from the
seminary to the practical problems of parish life. Another concern is for the beginning church executive,
moving from the business world or from a parish into
an administrative responsibility in the church. A third
is for the new ecumenical executive who leaves a parish
to assume an administrative post in an ecumenical
structure. In these pages I have tried to summarize
from my reading and experience practical insights concerning the church, its mission, the nature of community, and the mechanisms and techniques for planning,
administration, and evaluation that seem pertinent and
helpful.

Ecumenopolis

This word is borrowed from Dr. Constantine Doxiadis, noted Greek planner and futurist. Dr. Doxiadis used the word to mean "the world as a community." That concept is a significant one—"world community" is our concern also. However, as I use the word, the first part "ecumen" refers to the church—one church. "Menopolis" means community. "Metropolis" could also have been used, since metropolis is one of the important emerging realities in the U.S.A. However, there are other important communities in America that are not metropolitan and "menopolis" serves a more inclusive purpose. *Ecumenopolis* in this book means "one church, in mission, in community."

U.S.A.

The church in community in the U.S.A. is my subject because this is the "turf" with which I am familiar. The principles may apply to other countries as well, and persons familiar there will know how best to make application or necessary adaptations to their situations.

H. CONRAD HOYER

One Church

There Is One Church
of Jesus Christ
in All the World!

The statement seems utterly absurd to the practical observer. He sees hundreds of churches—thousands of them! Almost every village has half a dozen. The policeman on the corner of First and Main Street can direct the stranger to the Presbyterian church, to the Lutheran church, to the Roman Catholic church, or to the Baptist church, but ask him, "Where is the one church of Jesus Christ?" and he will shake his head, shrug his shoulders, and comment, "No such church in this town, or at least I haven't heard of any." This is "the ecumenical scandal on Main Street" which Dr. William Cate writes about.[1]

The *Yearbook of American Churches* for 1971 lists 230 religious bodies with 322,088 related parishes or congregations. Limit the data to specifically Christian bodies and the numbers are reduced only slightly to 220 Christian bodies and 315,747 parishes or congregations. Even this is only a partial picture, for many smaller groups have never become part of the reporting process. There are also thousands of local, regional, or national church activities which claim to represent some aspect of churchly expression.

The mass of emperical data shouts: "Many churches! Many churches!" As a practical church administrator I have had to deal with that data for twenty-eight years. Yet when I undertake to write this book I begin with the premise that there is *one church of Jesus Christ in all the world.* Further, I insist that this *one church* is a reality, not only in the imagination of the theologian or in my wish and dream, but in the real world of time and place. Beyond this, I will indicate that only as *one church* can the church of Jesus Christ really discover her mission and seriously address that mission in the world.

It is beyond the scope of this chapter to present a comprehensive, analytical treatment of the unity question. Fortunately, Dr. Hans Küng and others have done this for us. A bibliography of pertinent literature on the subject is included as an appendix. I can give only a broad-sweep summary here.

GROWS OUT OF SCRIPTURE

The premise of *one church of Jesus Christ* has substantial support in the Scriptures. The ecumenical text from the High Priestly prayer serves as a beginning for this review: "That they may all be one; even as thou, Father, art in me, and I in thee, that they also may be in us, so that the world may believe that thou hast sent me" (John 17:21). Clearly the Lord was concerned about unity, and he prays that his followers should be joined to each other like Father and Son are united—also that they may be "in us."

The Apostle Paul both assumes and affirms the concept of one church under one Lord. Thus he writes, "There is one body and one Spirit, just as you were called to the one hope that belongs to your call, one Lord, one faith, one baptism, one God and Father of

us all, who is above all and through all and in all"
(Ephesians 4:4-5). Noting that the verse does not say
one church, Dr. Visser 't Hooft, former General Secretary
of the World Council of Churches, commented concerning the omission: "The reason is surely that the oneness
of the church is so obvious to the New Testament generation that it need not be explicitly stated." [2]

The apostle resolves the paradox of *one church* over
against the reality of many and diverse expressions of it
by describing the church as an organism: one body,
under one head. That the churches appeared quite different did not upset Paul. He seemed not at all concerned
about uniformity. In the body image (variously stated:
Ephesians 4:5; Romans 12:5; 1 Corinthians 12:12-26)
Paul accepted diversity of expression, and even seemed
to regard it as a necessity. In 1 Corinthians 12 the differences are likened to different members of a body—
eye, hand, foot—with different functions to perform. Paul
insists that although the parts are different and have
different functions they are interdependent members of
one body, for there was only one body. Christ is the head
of that body.

When party strife developed in the church because
people responded to different strong leaders, the apostle
asks, "What then is Apollos? What is Paul? Servants
through whom you believed" (1 Cor. 3:5).

When cultures seemed to divide the church Paul affirms: "There is neither Jew nor Greek, there is neither
slave nor free, there is neither male nor female, for you
are all one in Christ Jesus" (Gal. 3:28). The apostle
selected points of greatest cultural cleavage in his day
to emphasize that even these cannot divide the church.
Persons belonging to uniquely different cultural groups
belonged together in Christ, and therefore they belonged together in his church!

The body figure is only one of many images which the

New Testament uses to describe the church. "The bride of Christ," "the temple of God," "a holy nation," "God's own people," "Christ's flock," "the vine and the branches," "the household of God," are others. Scholars have counted ninety such images. Each one implies, sometimes affirms, and usually requires unity.

A Gift from God

The unity of the church of Jesus Christ is not something which men or institutions create. It is rather a gift from God. It is a part of the "nature of things." Like other natural gifts—gold, coal, oil—it is there; it is up to us to discover it; we cannot make it. It is gross presumption on the part of the geologist or the prospector to pretend that he creates the gold, or the coal, or the oil! So too the unity of the church; it is God's gift; it is a part of the nature of his church; it is up to us to discover it!

The unity of the church is found *in Christ*, nowhere else! All the images about the church suggest this. He is the head; he is the husband; he is the Lord. When we discover him and give allegiance to him, then we find the church; then we find the unifying relations with others who are *in Christ* as well. We are members; there are millions of other members; these members are different in age, in color, in language, in education, in culture, in interests, in abilities. Through faith we are all members of one body, the church of Jesus Christ, for *there is only one body!*

AFFIRMED BY CREEDS

The historic creeds of Christendom were developed in times of intense theological controversy, and unity was one of the issues in those controversies. As faithful witnesses to the Scriptures these creeds strongly reaffirm the unity theme: *one church of Jesus Christ in all the world.* The Nicene Creed reads: "I believe in one, holy catholic and Apostolic Church." The Apostles' Creed, written centuries later, says it again: "I believe in the Holy Spirit, the Holy catholic Church, the Communion of Saints. . . . " It matters not that a few denominations have changed the word "catholic" to "Christian" for use in their liturgies. "Christian" is usually marked with an asterisk and "catholic" appears in the footnote. Whether "catholic" or "Christian," the definite article before the word accents *one church.* Nowhere do the creeds speak of "holy Christian churches." They reaffirm the premise: *One church of Jesus Christ in all the world.*

SUPPORTED BY COMMUNIONS

"Una Sancta" sang the choirs from ten church colleges at the festival service climaxing the organizing convention of The American Lutheran Church, April 24, 1960. I was one of the ten thousand worshipers in the Minneapolis auditorium at that great service. Thrilled by the music I was equally impressed by the focus on "Una Sancta"—*One Holy Church.* The message of the cantata was clear: one Lord, one church, one mission. Half of the words of the cantata were direct quotations from the King James' translation of the Scriptures with a few poetic variations. The unity theme came to a climax when the 500-voice choir sang: *"There is neither Jew, nor Greek, there is neither bond nor free, there is neither male nor female: for ye are all one in Christ Jesus. There is one body and one spirit, even as ye are called in one hope of your calling: One God and Father of all, who is above all, and through all, and in you all."* This cantata ought to be used more often as an art form for ecumenical celebration.[3]

In celebrating the merger of four different Lutheran

church bodies the festival cantata did not center on that event, but rather on the greater reality—one holy church —about which that significant merger event was only token and symbol.

Dr. Fredrik Schiotz, while president of The American Lutheran Church, called my attention to the cantata as an official affirmation of his church on the unity question. Official positions of a number of other churches and church organizations were gathered for this chapter. Though extremely pertinent, this material proved too extensive for inclusion in this chapter. It has been added as an appendix. The reader will want to note the material carefully. Not all churches say the same thing in the same words. However, through the rich variety of rhetoric comes the common refrain "Una Sancta" as the Scriptures declare it, as the creeds witness to it, and as young voices sang it in Minneapolis.

UNDERSCORED BY ECUMENICAL AGENCIES

Ecumenical agencies naturally stress the unity theme. The Oberlin Conference, sponsored by the U.S. Committee of the World Council of Churches in 1957, studied "The Nature of the Unity We Seek." In its message to the churches it affirms:

> We have known a common joy in the unity we now possess, we have also felt a common sorrow over the continuing fact of our separations one from another. We acknowledge the one Lord; we also own the peril of calling him "Lord, Lord," and failing to do the things he has commanded. We cannot forget that his prayer for the unity of his followers remains unfulfilled. Although some of our divisions arise out of loyalty to truth that we now see, we must acknowledge that Christ calls us to a fuller comprehension of truth and more obedient service. To proclaim that Christ is the one Lord is to give him preeminence over all else—over our most cherished traditions. This we have not done.

Yet God gives us hope. We do not see clearly the path that God has set before us, but we are sure that he is leading us, and that at Oberlin he has given us new light.

In this light we see that the Church is God's Church and that the unity is his unity. This unity, we believe, is to be:

—A unity in Christ who died for us, is risen, regnant, and will come again to gather together all things in his judgment and grace;

—A unity in adoration of God—one offering of wonder, love and praise;

—A unity of declared faith, sounding the vast Amen of the whole Church's believing life through all the centuries;

—A unity of bearing one another's burdens and sharing one another's joys;

—A unity in which every ministry is a ministry of and for all the members, bound together in a worshiping and sacramental community;

—A unity in mission to the world, originating with, sustained by and offered to the one Christ, and conducted with such transparency of love and faithfulness that the world will believe on him;

—A unity possessing rich variety in worship, life and organization.[4]

At New Delhi in 1961 the World Council of Churches approved the St. Andrew's statement, developed by the Central Committee of the World Council of Churches at its meeting in St. Andrews, Scotland, in 1960. The statement reads:

We believe that the unity which is both God's Will and His Gift to His Church is being made visible, as all in each place who are baptized into Jesus Christ and confess Him as Lord and Saviour are brought by the Holy Spirit into one fully-committed fellowship, holding the one apostolic faith, preaching the one Gospel, breaking the one bread, joining in common prayer, and having a

corporate life reaching out in witness and service to all;
and at the same time are united with the whole Christian
fellowship in all places and all ages in such ways that
ministry and members are accepted by all, and that all
can act and speak together as occasion requires for the
tasks to which God calls His people.[5]

The Preamble to the Constitution of the National
Council of Churches sets the pattern for state, metropolitan and local councils. That preamble reads:

Under the Providence of God communions which confess
Jesus Christ as Divine Lord and Savior, in order more
fully to manifest oneness in Him, do now create an inclusive cooperative agency of Christian churches of the
United States of America to show forth their unity and
mission in specific ways and to bring the churches into
living contact with one another for fellowship, study,
and cooperative action.

A few councils go beyond that. The Church Council
of Greater Seattle in the preamble to its new constitution
(November 16, 1969) declares:

God calls the Church into being through Jesus Christ,
to live in His name in all areas of the human situation—
there to testify who God is, and to show forth, in and
by the life of the Church, how God works through
community to meet the pressing needs of the human
condition.

We, confessing Jesus Christ as Lord, the Lord of this
metropolitan area, and as Savior, the Savior of men in
their actual situation, and standing in the long line of
men reaching down from the Hebrew prophets, testify
that God is calling the Church in Greater Seattle into
creative involvement in the life, work, and play of this
metropolis.

We testify to the brokenness of life in this community.
The dehumanizing effects of separations, fears, tensions,
and present dangers are evident on every hand, and now
threaten to destroy what "community" does exist.

We confess that the Church is broken, in its separation searching for an effective vehicle through which it may plan and work as one people of God in showing forth here the Good News of Christ in the midst of human need.

Through what God is doing in both Church and World, He is calling the Church to unity in order that its common life may bear effective witness to His power and love, His justice and righteousness.

In subscribing to this Constitution, we, the regional denominational judicatories, the local congregations, the councils of churches, and the para-church structures of this metropolis, do acknowledge now that we are essential parts of the Church of Jesus Christ in this place—and so are part of the problem as well as essential to the unifying, healing purpose and process to which we are called in this time.

CONFUSION CONTINUES

We wish we could remain forever on the mountain top, basking in the harmonious rhetoric of denominational and ecumenical affirmations. However, this book has a practical purpose and it must deal with the real world of the U.S.A. where there are more than 200 separate Christian denominations and 313,000 separate congregations. It must deal with the fact that in "Our Town, U.S.A." there are four Christian congregations belonging to four different denominations, worshiping in four separate church buildings, located on four corners of the town square, and no two congregations have more than a "nodding acquaintance" with each other! Such is church life U.S.A. in the moon-landing decade of the 20th century! *Where is the one church of Jesus Christ in the U.S.A.?* Indeed!

How is it possible to have this affirmed loyalty to Scripture and to creeds, and these excellent declarations about the unity of the church on the one hand, and at the same time have this shocking fragmentation of churches on the other? It is a scandal and no one tries to justify it. One can, however, explain it in terms of history, geography, ethnic and cultural loyalties, strong personalities, and honest theological differences.

Many of the denominational groupings reflect a carry-over from the migration movements of a century ago. Immigrants from Europe brought their church patterns and loyalties with them and established national-cultural enclaves in communities where they settled. This included the church. Thus there remain a number of Dutch reformed and Swiss reformed colonies. Two such colonies adjacent to one another in South Dakota continue their separate churches though both churches use only English in their services of worship, and both churches are now served by the same pastor. Many of the apparent Lutheran divisions before World War II can be explained in the same way.

The awakening and revival movements of a century ago gave birth to many separatist groups, sometimes on the basis of theology or temperament, at other times on the basis of geography or strong personalities. These separations lingered institutionally, long after the movements had run their course. This could easily happen because the country was large, communication was limited, and religious happenings in Missouri and North Carolina could develop in parallel fashion, flourish, and institutionalize before they encountered one another. Many church separations resulted from the social and political cleavages which led to the Civil War.

Not all church fragmentation in America can be explained by history, sociology, geography, or personality. There are deep and serious theological differences as well, and it is not a service to the one church of Jesus Christ, or to the Lord of that church, to think or to write as if these differences were not real. Many of these differences have been with us since the time of the apostles; others arose in the Middle Ages. Science and technology have introduced still others. Differences on these newer issues are often as great within a denomination as between denominations. So far as this chapter is concerned we acknowledge the reality of theological differences. In line with the basic premise of this chapter, however, we question whether two Christians or two Christian communions, each claiming allegiance to Jesus Christ as Lord and Savior, can in good conscience write each other off, or dare to refuse to relate to each other, since both are members of *one body*.

Admittedly, there must be some criteria for judgment. A criteria that has gained general acceptance in recent years is the "evangelical principle." According to this principle we recognize as brothers for Christian relationship purposes those who "acknowledge Jesus Christ as Lord and Savior." The principle in no way sets aside the necessity and propriety of establishing appropriate human relations and institutional relations with others who do not accept that lordship. It does set a criteria for identifying the *one church of Jesus Christ*.

SOME MENDING TRENDS

The Christian movement in America has been divisive, but there are also mending trends. Significant reformations have taken place during the past thirty years. The breach between North and South has largely been healed. In 1961 the Evangelical and Reformed Church, and the Congregational-Christian Churches merged to form the United Church of Christ. This was a significant development because the merging bodies represented different national backgrounds, different cultural traditions, and quite different church government practices.

The Presbyterian Church U.S.A. merged with the United Presbyterian Church to form the United Presbyterian Church in the U.S.A. in 1957. Lutheran re-formations have been in process since the turn of the century. A major development united four bodies to form The American Lutheran Church in 1960, and four other bodies formed the Lutheran Church in America in 1962. These two larger bodies are related to each other and to the Lutheran Church—Missouri Synod through the Lutheran Council in the U.S.A. The Evangelical-United Brethren Church united with the Methodist Church to form the United Methodist Church in 1968. Nine major Protestant church bodies have been in process of merger negotiations since 1960 in a movement known as COCU. Originally the letters stood for "Consultation on Church Union." In 1968 the movement had progressed so that a new name was adopted and the same letters were used to signify the "Church of Christ Uniting."

At Local Levels Also

While these combinations were taking place at national levels, changes were also apparent at local levels. Exact documentation is difficult because no one has really kept track of the unifications and regroupings in local and city communities. Yet some developments are clear:

1. In hundreds of communities, neighbor congregations have merged to form one church. This has been necessary in many towns or rural areas because population has declined by 20 percent or more in rural America, and new transportation possibilities have reduced the necessity for "convenience location" churches. Mergers have been just as necessary in larger city areas as the population in many city neighborhoods have changed completely within a decade. Most mergers of

congregations have taken place between congregations of the same denomination. This has been easier because it has involved the surrender of fewer loyalties. It has been facilitated by the merging of denominations at the national level.

There have also been mergers across denominational lines as local congregations and their denominational leaders have seen the futility of maintaining competitive programs where one congregation would do better than two, or three, or four. Local people usually make the choice as to which denomination they should relate to, though this decision is made in close cooperation with the leadership of the denominations involved. In some cases congregations have chosen to relate to a denomination not represented by any of the merging congregations. A few congregations merge and affiliate nowhere, remaining independent community churches.

2. A variation is to form a united church. In this arrangement, a congregation affiliates with one denomination, but with a membership provision so that persons may join the congregation and still retain denominational loyalty and affiliation with some other denomination. Arrangements are made to provide for the denominational ministries which the local congregation cannot provide. (For instance, Communion to Episcopalians, Missouri Lutherans, or Orthodox.) United churches have existed for many years in a number of towns in Utah, but they can be found elsewhere as well.

3. Congregations have yoked into larger parishes or cluster parishes. In this approach each congregation retains its autonomy, its denominational affiliation, perhaps its own building, but it joins with others for common action in areas of joint concern such as education, leadership training, youth ministry, community services. Staff of the larger parish share their special skills. The

office equipment is also shared, and sometimes a common office is used for all. A larger parish board provides the organizational framework for such a program.

4. The development of union churches, where two congregations of different denominations use the same building, was a popular development in rural and village Pennsylvania a century ago and it has been found elsewhere, as well. Many of these shared building arrangements are now being dissolved in Pennsylvania, but new forms of the same approach are developing. Thus the New Community of Columbia, Maryland, has a joint building used by Jews, Roman Catholics, and several Protestant groups. Broadway Congregational Church in downtown Manhattan, New York, has recently disposed of its building and has arranged to rent facilities from a nearby Roman Catholic Church.

5. Dual affiliation is another possibility. The best illustration of this is the prestigious Riverside Church, on Riverside Drive, New York, which is related to the American Baptist Convention and to the United Church of Christ. A number of Baptist congregations have dual affiliation with the American Baptist Convention and the Southern Baptist Convention.

Although this list is incomplete, it indicates some of the stirrings at local levels in the direction of unity. Very often those developments are prompted more by necessity or the recognized economies which result, than by a concern for expression of the one church of Jesus Christ. However, we believe that sometimes these things happen because people have learned something about the one church of Jesus Christ, and because they have been concerned to lessen the scandal of our extreme church separatism in the place where they live.

Mobility of population has also broken the sharp denominational differentiations of 30 years ago. As people move from neighborhood to neighborhood (at an average, people move once every five years) they make their church membership choices more on the basis of the convenience of the church location, or on the quality of a local church program, than on its denominational label or its theological position. Thus every congregation in a city or suburban community has people in its membership who grew up in a dozen other denominational traditions. Members in Reformed churches were confirmed in Lutheran churhes; lay leaders in Methodist congregations grew up in Baptist traditions; Presbyterian elders are sons of Episcopal bishops. This challenges the official differentiations that were so highly accented in the separatist era.

Furthermore, the current position of the Vatican (see appendix) has started a whole new series of dialogues between Roman Catholic churches and churches of Protestant and Orthodox traditions. The Week of Prayer for Christian Unity has captured the interest and attention of vast segments of the country, and special observances with major lay participation have been held in hundreds of communities. New mechanisms for faith and order studies, for practical cooperation, for common address to community problems, for theological education, are erupting everywhere.

Lay Movements

Many lay people, unimpressed by the splintering movements among Christian churches, have related to each other in other ways to carry out their Christian responsibilities. Thus, the Sunday school associations of a century ago were lay-oriented, and non-denominational, though with zealous Christian commitment. By now that movement is almost forgotten, but in the early 20th century there were 2,000 city or county

Sunday school associations. The YMCA and the YWCA
have survived as non-denominational lay-oriented movements with long histories of service concern. Church
Women United, with a national staff and a national
focus but with emphasis also on local units and responsibility in neighborhood areas, is a contemporary lay
movement which emphasizes united Christian witness
and action for all Christians. Hundreds of local lay
groups of men, students, youth, have been formed as
Christians in local communities join hands for various
purposes from praying together at breakfast to cleaning
up polluted air, water, and natural habitats, to elimi-
nating racial discrimination in jobs and housing.

MOVEMENTS TOWARD COOPERATION

"Maybe churches can't unite, but at least they should
be able to cooperate with one another if they have as
much in common as they say they have." This is a solid
and logical conclusion of many practical church people.
As a result cooperation has become one of the major
mending movements on the horizon.

Church cooperation often happens because there is
no other way to get tasks done. In today's complex
world no church can go it alone, really. The chapters
that follow will deal with this practical side of the question. This chapter affirms that churches should not go
it alone even if they could, for they belong together as
members of one holy, catholic church. Cooperation is
one of the ways in which they try to go it together.

Since the conciliar pattern provides the most common
form for interchurch cooperation, it is described here in
more detail. Most of the organized conciliar interchurch
expressions are called councils of churches. However,
since that name has become a barrier to some, a dozen
other designations are now in use: conference of church-

es; association of churches; federation of churches; ecumenical bureaus; metropolitan area church boards; metropolitan interchurch agencies, to name only a few.

Conciliar agencies are organized to enable the churches:

1. To discover the unity they have in Christ Jesus;

2. To make that discovered unity manifest to the world;

3. To discover their mission in time and place;

4. To devise means to carry forward that mission in faithful obedience to their Lord.

5. To enable the churches to do those things together that they ought to do together, that they must do together if they are to be done at all, and to do those things together that they can do together more effectively or efficiently than they can do them separately.

Not every conciliar agency does all these things, by any means. Some forget the first one entirely—that is one of the concerns of this chapter. Others try to do the second task without addressing themselves to the first one! Items 3, 4, and 5 will be discussed later.

Admittedly, the conciliar movement in the United States has not measured up to its potential. It too has been partial and fragmented. To illustrate, there are three national conciliar expressions in this country: the National Council of Churches in the U.S.A., the National Council of Evangelicals, and the American Council. Organized state councils exist in all states except Mississippi and Alabama, but some are very weak. There are conciliar ecumenical structures in 700 metropolitan areas, cities, or counties; 210 of these have paid staff.[6]

The problem of how to relate one level of cooperative expression to other levels and how to relate cooperative units at the same level to each other has not been resolved. Furthermore, these cooperative units have been only parts, sometimes minority parts, of the total Christian community in a region.

Progress is being made in both directions and since 1965 conciliar structures have moved to include a much larger segment of the Christian community in the areas of their service. This has been largely due to the new possibilities for relationship with Roman Catholic churches after Vatican II. By 1971 Roman Catholic dioceses were in full membership in eleven state conciliar agencies. Roman Catholic dioceses or parishes were in full membership in fifty metropolitan or city ecumenical agencies, and they were in effective program cooperation in two hundred other regional or local ecumenical expressions. The outreach to include Roman Catholics has also opened avenues for more Orthodox and wider Protestant participation.

Doing things together will be discussed later. Suffice it to say here that churches are relating to one another and discovering one another through various forms of conciliar expression.

Is cooperation enough? Or is it only one more of the mending trends which ameliorates the scandal of church separation just a little and provides a half-way place to rest, an excuse for churches not to go beyond that? Dr. Forrest Knapp raises this interesting question in his book, *Church Cooperation: Dead-end Street or Highway to Unity.* He concludes:

> I believe the churches can make it a highway if they will. Councils of churches may prove to be, for some churches, a half-way house which those churches will decide to make their permanent cooperative residence instead of pressing upward to the peak. But if there is unquenchable zeal for unity, cooperation in councils will be an aid of importance, not in their net effect a hindrance. The decision rests with the churches themselves.[7]

It is very clear that low levels of cooperation are not enough, and a grave danger in the conciliar movement is that it plateaus too easily. Ten congregations belonging to six denominations get together to do three things cooperatively through a council of churches. Then they settle for that, rejoice in it, and go no farther for ten years. The fact that there are thirty other congregations in the city and fifteen of these belong to ten other denominations does not seem to be relevant. Furthermore, dozens of other tasks could have been undertaken if they had been undertaken together, but the churches settled for three and stopped there! They plateau too easily!

If we are to pursue the cooperative route, then we should set a high goal, like: "to do all things together as one church of Jesus Christ except those things which in good conscience we must do separately," as the Lund assembly of the World Council suggested. Not impressed with the efficiency of centralized bureaucracies I would add that congregations or denominations should do separately, but not without relation to other churches, those things which can be handled more effectively or efficiently separately than together.

However, all things should be done in the perspective of *one church of Jesus Christ in all the world.* Cooperation is not only a quest for unity, or a highway to unity; it is an expression of unity as well.

WHAT OF THE FUTURE?

Where will all this lead us? Back to the opening sentence of this chapter: *one church of Jesus Christ in all the world!* What this will mean for tomorrow, I cannot say. At least we cannot rest where we are! *One church* calls for more reaching out to others who likewise profess the faith; it calls for new discoveries of common bonds and new working relations; it calls for new attempts at faithful witness as well as new efforts at honest listening. It calls for more cooperation. Union now? Or in the future? Who knows where the Spirit will lead us. Undoubtedly, many unions will come, and should come, as the Spirit leads. Perhaps total union in the organizational sense will never come. Perhaps it should not. The unity in Christ *has* come; it is here; Christians and Christian churches need to discover it, become a part of it, and declare to one another and to the world that there is *one church of Jesus Christ in all the world!* To this we are called!

CHAPTER 2

One Mission

Mission is discovering what God is calling his church to be and to do in the human community of time and place, and doing that to which she is called.

The definition is related to the understanding of the church as set forth in the first chapter: God's church; one in Christ; under his lordship. God has a will for his church. He calls it into being and into service. It becomes our business as responsible members of his church to discover that call and to respond in obedience. That is the church's primary business; that is our business as faithful members of his one body.

Admittedly, not every religious institution with a Christian label is concerned with mission according to this definition. At least, not always! That is the institutional problem of the churches. If churches are not concerned about mission in these terms, then they are off the track, as Christian churches, and this chapter aims to call them back. The church of Jesus Christ is always in this kind of business: *discovering and doing what God calls her to be and do!*

CAN WE KNOW?

The definition assumes that it is possible to discover God's will. If it were not possible there would be no point in trying. Then we could dismiss the divine dimension of the church and settle for the church as one of the

better-than-average human institutions trying to provide
some rationale, solace, and purpose for man during his
brief earthly sojourn from the cradle to the grave.

We assume and affirm that the church of Jesus Christ
is more than that! The church is of God, and under a
divine mandate. Further, we assume and affirm that it
is possible to discern, in part at least, what God's will
and purpose is for the church. We say it is possible; we
do not say that it is easy. I have little confidence in
those who claim to have hot line connections with the
Lord of heaven, so that they can know quite precisely
at any given time what the will of the Lord is. I would
treasure the gift if it were possible; I do not possess it.
For most people, God is more often the *Deus Abscon-
ditus*—the hidden God. At best we see through a glass,
darkly. Yet he does make his will and his way known.
We can find if we seek, so we must seek. This book aims
to aid earnest Christians who have responsibility in his
church to search for that will and that way. Usually we
will not see the full road, and we should not expect a
full and clear vision. We will get some light as we seek,
and only as we respond in faith and obedience to that
which is given will we get more light for the path
ahead. In this sense Christians and Christian churches
are like Abraham of old; we hear a call and respond
in faith, not knowing just where it will lead.

CALLED TO BE

Our definition of mission includes both "being" and
"doing." The church of Jesus Christ is just as much
called to achieve a certain stance and character of
"being" as it is called to undertake certain courses of
action. Not more, but just as much! Furthermore, the
right *being* often becomes a prerequisite to effective
doing. Many actions of the church fall short of their

intended purposes because in zealous concern for action the churches forget who they are—the church of Jesus Christ—and they forget to act that way. If churches become just one more of the "do good" institutions in our society, they should not be surprised if they have no more effect than other "do good" groups.

It is interesting to note that the Nicene Creed suggests four characteristics of being for the church without a single reference to doing. That creed describes the church as: one, holy, catholic (universal), apostolic. This is an excellent summary witness to the Scriptures. It is only a summary, and Christians and Christian churches need to pause with the sacred writings long enough to learn the full picture of what the Word really says the church should be. To suggest this is to sound a call to radical renewal for all the churches. So be it! Even a casual study of the Bible exposes the gap between churches as we know them, and the church as it is pictured in the New Testament. Although the churches in Corinth and Ephesus in New Testament days fell short too, this is no excuse for us. The sacred writers called those churches to repentance and renewal. God calls his churches today through his Word to be renewed that they may become his church: one, holy, catholic, apostolic!

One, holy, catholic, apostolic—indeed! These four descriptive adjectives from the Nicene Creed can be a starting point for a renewal call. Even undertaking any two of them as a beginning would be pretty radical! The 4th chapter of Ephesians could serve as a rallying text, reinforced by the 12th chapter of Romans!

These references suggest only a few of the many calls to be. Very much of the New Testament is concerned with direct or indirect guidance concerning how Christians and Christian churches are called to be in relation to God, to other members, to neighbors, and to the world.

The right being is important to mission because Christian presence is often the most important, and sometimes its only possible means. In almost every case being either reinforces or contradicts what we say and do.

CALLED TO DO

Since Americans are action-oriented it is fortunate for churches in America that the church is also called to do. Scriptures clearly indicate what we should do. Hear the great commission: "Go, therefore, and make disciples of all nations, baptizing them in the name of the Father, and of the Son, and of the Holy Spirit, teaching them to observe all I have commanded you; and lo, I am with you always, to the close of the age" (Matthew 28:19-20). The Book of Acts says the same thing in terms of witness: "But ye shall receive power when the Holy Spirit has come upon you; and you shall be my witnesses in Jerusalem, and in Judea and Samaria and to the end of the earth" (Acts 1:8). The judgment story in Matthew 24 points to action directions: "feed the hungry," "clothe the naked." The Sermon on the Mount (Matthew 5–7) suggests other things to do like "turn the other cheek," and "bear good fruit." The Parable of the Good Samaritan makes its point concerning help to the neighbor in distress. People are less familiar with "As you have opportunity, let us do good unto all men, and especially to those who are of the household of faith" (Galatians 6:10), or "if your enemy is hungry, feed him, if he is thirsty give him to drink" (Romans 12:20). The Old Testament also sounds its call in passages like, "Let justice roll down like water, and righteousness like a mighty stream" (Amos 5:24). Such a call to action speaks loudly to this generation. This is only a start; almost every page of the Bible sets forth some call "to do."

The many and varied calls to mission in the Scriptures have been summarized in five Greek words.

Kerygma—witness. In mission terms *kerygma* means the full witness concerning the grace and truth of Jesus Christ, to all men, everywhere. It includes witness in both word and action. The church is called to witness!

Koinonia—fellowship. The church calls those who respond to the witness to a fellowship with each other. We call this the gathered church. It is the beloved community. The church nurtures the believers in and through this fellowship.

Diakonia—service. The Christian fellowship ministers in loving service to its members and to all mankind as a response to the Christian experience of God's grace and truth in Christ.

Didache—teaching. This is a major ministry of the church and it is one of the ways of witness, of nurture, and of service.

Leiturgia—worship. This means much more than the form and activity in which Christians participate in a service of worship in the church on a Sunday morning. That too is worship. However, in the mission sense *leiturgia* means the over-all orientation for the way and spirit of the church at work. All church work is done in the spirit of adoration, praise, thanksgiving, intercession, supplication, submission. This is the liturgy of the godly life. This is *leiturgia!*

One hardly need comment concerning these different elements of the call to do except to say that all are involved. Mission perspective gets too narrow when any one of them is left out.

The call to witness is clear. Isn't that what preaching is all about? Isn't that why we send missionaries? The witness in action, by giving a cup of cold water, or by championing the cause of the poor before a legislative sub-committee, is also part of the witness concerning God's grace and truth.

The church that witnesses also gathers and includes in its fellowship all who respond to that witness. This fellowship is "the communion of saints"; it is "the people of God." Through this fellowship the church nurtures, sustains, and enriches the faithful. This is a chief purpose of church membership, of church worship, of church school teaching, and of the various inter-personal encounters in church auxiliaries.

The people of God always serve in love. They serve especially the household of faith, but they serve all men as well. The church must serve. That is part of her nature. Just as the Lord "came not to be ministered unto but to minister" so the church, which is his body, reaches out in ministries of service to men and to society everywhere. Children's homes, homes for the aged, hospitals, institutions for the handicapped, schools in out-of-the-way places—these are not accidental developments in the church of Jesus Christ. They are essentials! So are the world-wide ministries of resettlement, food and clothing distribution, as well as programs of self-help in the ghetto or in some far-off South Sea Island. So also are the efforts to secure legislative reforms to provide justice and equality of opportunity in our society.

The commission to "teach them to observe all that I have commanded you" (Matthew 28:20) has been heard and heeded well by the churches. Church schools, vacation schools, released time classes, confirmation classes, lay institutes, retreats, church colleges, indicate only a few of the ways the churches have responded to this element of mission. The sermon and the whole structure of the service of worship are also means of teaching.

Leiturgia indicates the spirit and provides the unifying element of all that Christians do. Paul's admonition to the Corinthians: "Whether you eat or drink or whatever you do, do all to the glory of God" (1 Cor. 10:31), becomes a description of the liturgy of a godly life. Witness, fellowship, service, teaching, find a unifying center in that kind of living worship.

IN THE HUMAN SITUATION

The Scriptures have been our source and guide thus far. Anyone seriously concerned about God's will and his call to his church in our day, needs to know what he willed and what he called his people to be and to do in an earlier day. This is where we begin the quest. However, God is not calling us to be and to do in that long-gone distant past. He calls us to be his people and to be his church, and to do his work in the world and in the human situation of today. In fact, *the specifics of mission—the specific things which God calls us to do—are always discovered in the human situation of time and place.* The italics set forth one of the axioms of this book. We perceive God's will in today's situations on the basis of the revelation of his will in earlier situations. But the specifics of his call are found in the situations of time and place—the *now* of history. Therefore, one must know both the Word and the world to perceive God's will and his call for our day. To study one without the other will lead to faulty conclusions because one will not have adequate input to perceive aright the nature of God's call for this time and place.

Admittedly this becomes an on-going task. We can never know all there is to know either in the Word or in the world, but we can grow in knowledge of both, and as we grow, and as we bring the knowledge of both together, we can perceive better what God calls us to be and to do here and now.

CHAPTER 3

Mission in Community

The church of Jesus Christ is always in mission in the human community of time and place. The church and the nature of its mission are only theoretical until they come to focus in human community—the arena in which the church exercises her mission of being and doing.

WHAT IS COMMUNITY?

But what is community? The question is critical; the answers are not clear. These uncertainties have created major conceptual problems for today's society. They also present tactical problems for churches.

In the early part of the 20th century community was understood to be a geographical area, with a natural center, that reached out about as far as a team and wagon could go and return in a day. The radius was described as "the team-haul." Boundaries were not absolute, often modified by natural barriers such as rivers or mountains, but these variations did not change the principle. Community was identified with a piece of geography. It was assumed that most meaningful relationships were confined to that limited geography. This was largely true. People spent most of their lives within the confines of the defined area. Within those boundaries they had opportunity for face-to-face contacts. Here they could visit other people within a day's journey. Here they purchased their supplies and disposed of their products. Church, school, and social life were related to that geography. Here people found their marriage partners. Within those boundaries people were dependent on one another and strong loyalties developed. Strong rivalries also developed, for all was not paradise!

Even today some hollows of Appalachia or towns of New England show many of the same characteristics, and one can find remnants of such typical communities in rural sections of mid-America, Pennsylvania or New York. However, for the most part this kind of community is gone, even in the more sparsely settled areas of America. It certainly does not fit metropolis. We may have some nostalgia about it, and we may try to hold on to parts of the old if we can, but this is not America in the 1970s! Communication, transportation, vocational mobility, urbanization, and the emergence of metropolis make such a geographical concept of community totally inadequate.

Unfortunately, no one has developed a contemporary concept that fits the new facts. Instead, we have made ad hoc adaptations and modernizations of the old. We still think of community in terms of face-to-face contacts, related to a homogeneous piece of geography. We assume that geographical proximity provides the primary basis for peoples' relationships to one another. While the facts of life do not square with the concept, we have no other adequate framework to which we can relate. Lacking an alternative, students of sociology write of "the eclipse of community." [1] People in the 1970s need to relate to each other more than ever before, for they are more interdependent than ever. However, these relationships are not based on community in the early 20th century terms.

What then is community? In today's world *community*

*is any continuing, meaningful relationship between peo-
ple for their mutual benefit.* "Benefit" in this definition
must be understood broadly to mean physical protection,
economic security, spiritual enrichment, mental stimula-
tion, moral support, cultural advance, and similar inter-
changes.

This concept of community accents relationships rather
than geography. The benefits, however, are much the
same as those claimed for the earlier community concept.
The definition does not deny or ignore geography. It
allows rather for a pluralism of communities, recognizing
that these "meaningful relationships for mutual benefit"
may exist at many geographical levels. Other "meaningful relationships for mutual benefit" exist which have
little to do with geography.

This concept of different levels is not entirely new.
Township-county-state-nation governmental structure
provides a tacit recognition of it in political terms. For
school purposes townships have been further divided
into districts. Thus we have inherited at least five distinct
political levels for different purposes of government, and
the divisions have been with us for more than a century.
Church bodies usually have two organizational structures between the national body and local congregations, though there is no common agreement as to the
words used to designate these intermediate structures.
Our definition recognizes each of these levels in either
church or state as a possible valid community—"a relationship for mutual benefit."

However, the definition implies more than that. Modern community may not fit these neatly defined boundary systems, inherited from the past. They can be used
but they do not always provide the most valid or viable
units for meaningful relationship. To deal with the modern world the *regional concept* is a more flexible way of
viewing society.

As a concept, the region is like "X" in algebra—it may equal different things in different equations. In this sense it is unlike the arithmetic specifics: 2, or 5, or 57; or the geographical specifics: township, city, state. The region may equal any one of these. For one purpose the regional unit may be very small; for another purpose it may include half of the world. *The region may be defined as that geographical area which provides appropriate meaningful relationships with respect to a given purpose or concern.* Thus, the region may be different for smog control than for transportation, or education, or advertising. With the regional concept we can cross state lines or village boundaries without a single twinge of conscience if the occasion calls for it. The region need not even be a geographical area; it may be a cultural or interest region which has little to do with geography.

This may seem confusing to those accustomed to thinking in concrete geographical terms, just as algebra is confusing at first to those trained in arithmetic. However, when one adjusts to this understanding of community as "meaningful relationships for mutual benefit," the regional concept provides a helpful way of understanding the modern world, as well as the related units within it.

This is closer to U.S.A. in the 1970s. We need meaningful relationships at many geographical levels and in some non-geographical areas as well, and it is often difficult to determine which ones are the more important. For some situations the neighborhood is still primary; for other concerns a world-wide relationship may be the only meaningful one! For still others there is need for units in between.

My own situation is an illustration. I live in Bergenfield, New Jersey, a town of 32,000 people. Bergenfield is one of seventy towns in Bergen County, New Jersey, a county of 900,000 people. The county, in turn, is part of the North Jersey metropolis of 5,000,000 people. This again, is part of the New York-New Jersey-Connecticut metropolitan region of thirty-two counties in three states with a population of 20,000,000. Bergen County is a political sub-unit of the state of New Jersey, the Northeast geographical region, a part of the U.S.A., and a part of the world. I am a part of each of these communities. I derive benefits from each, have responsibilities to each, and have relationships at each level. For some purposes the town of Bergenfield is a primary community; for other purposes the metropolis is more meaningful; for still others the nation, or the world.

I am also a part of other communities that have little to do with geography. I belong to Trinity Lutheran congregation, Tenafly, New Jersey. I work for the National Council of Churches with offices in New York City, in a different state than my residence, thirteen miles from home. I travel to work in a car pool, a distinctly new community structure of modern metropolis. I spend three weeks a year in a "vacation community" at our home-on-the-river, near Phillips, Wisconsin, 1,200 miles from our New Jersey residence. I belong to the Association of Council Secretaries, a national professional organization. My family community is also important, even though the children are scattered across the nation. Distance does not break the bond, since all five children can be reached by telephone within five minutes, at a cost of less than $5.00! Furthermore, modern transportation makes it possible for the family to gather for special occasions, and I usually see them all, including the grandchildren, at least once every other year.

Everyone's list of community relationships will be different, to be sure, but a little reflection will indicate that many meaningful ties for mutual benefit reach beyond the team-haul boundaries, and some of these other ties are more significant than relationships within the neighborhood geography.

Thus, the static geographic concept of community does not fit today's needs, for it does not adequately describe the necessity and helpful relationships that man has with his fellowman in today's world. I have suggested a different concept of community that accents "meaningful relationships for mutual benefit." These exist at different levels, beginning with the neighborhood and extending to the whole world. Some of these relationships have little to do with geography. Some, like vacation communities, may be for only brief periods. The regional concept was introduced as a way of thinking about new meaningful relationships without the limitation of static boundary systems.

THAT'S WHERE MISSION IS TO BE FOUND

Why this extended sociological discourse about regions and community in a chapter concerned about the mission of the church? Because mission is *in community,* and unless we catch the multi-dimensional understanding of community in today's world we will fail to see the many dimensions of mission for the church. Instead, we will see mission only in terms of carefully bounded places—four walls of a local church, or a village, or a local neighborhood—and our understanding of mission will be limited to those local settings. As there are many levels of community, so there are also many levels of mission, for mission is in human community. Perhaps we should revise the statement to give the plural emphasis and say that *mission is in human communities at many different levels.*

RESPONSIBILITY AS LOCAL AS POSSIBLE

In its concern for mission the church begins with local communities and responsibility for them. An important mission axiom could be stated this way: *responsibility*

for mission should be as local as possible. If my neighbor
is ill and I can serve him, then it is neither proper nor
efficient for me to refer that responsibility to the visita-
tion committee of the congregation to which I belong.
If it is possible for me to do the mission task, then I
should do it. It can be that local! However many tasks
cannot be as local as the individual. If they are to be
done, they must be handled by the congregation. Other
tasks cannot be handled by a single congregation; if
they are to be done, they must be done by congregations
together in a village. Still other tasks are better handled
at the county level; others at the metropolitan level, or
a the state level. We repeat the axiom: *responsibility for
mission should be as local as possible.*

LEVELS OF MISSION

The prceding paragraph mentions different levels: individual, congregation, neighborhood, city, county,
metropolis, state. We might add nation, continent, and
world to that catalogue. Then there are sectors, trade
areas, functional planning areas, to mention only a few
other distinct and meaningful divisions.

This understanding of "levels" is a sequel to the multi-
dimensional understanding of community. It is not possible for many tasks to be done at the individual level,
or at the level of the local congregation. Other tasks
cannot be done at the state level. Therefore, in discovering what God is calling his church to be and to do, and
in deciding how and where to proceed, it is important
to recognize the different levels, to identify the appropriate level for action, and then to structure our response
at the level most appropriate to the task. We summarize
the principle in another axiom: *Efficient and effective
mission engagement depends upon identifying the appropriate level.* The corollary of this is that when we

fail to identify the level, or when we are not structured to address the task at that level and try to address it from some other level, we may spin wheels and get attention, but we do not get much accomplished.

Everyday experience offers plenty of examples. A local pastor and his congregation became concerned about police brutality in Jersey City, and sent representatives to the police department to protest. The police department listened to the delegation, but nothing much happened (the congregation was too local). The State Council of Churches likewise became aroused and sent representatives to the police department to declare its concern. This delegation was also heard but without much result (the state council was not local enough). It was only when the issue was identified as a Jersey City issue, and the churches of Jersey City became aroused and structured a response together as a total Christian community, that the police gave serious attention to their protests.

Hudson County, New Jersey, provides another example. The Christian Clergy Association of West New York (a city of 20,000 people) was concerned about the need for an adequate chaplaincy program in the institutions of Hudson County. The clergy association made several approaches to the county freeholders (county commissioners or supervisors in other states) over a period of three years, but without success. The association soon recognized that it received little attention because it was too local, and it therefore invited other clergy groups in other cities of the county to develop a joint approach to support this concern. Other groups were interested, but without a county church mechanism to address this and other county concerns, little progress was made, and it is doubtful that much will happen without a county structure.

On the other hand in Bergen County, North of Hudson County, there is a county council of churches. The same issue of chaplaincy services was raised with the freeholders in Bergen County a few years ago, and an excellent program is now in operation. It has developed so that the program employs a trained professional staff of five full-time and two part-time chaplains. This was a county level issue, addressed by the appropriate community, and the ministry was accomplished.

Admittedly many situations are not as simple and as clear as the police brutality issue in Jersey City or the chaplaincy need in Hudson County. We have oversimplified to illustrate the principle. In most areas some parts of the task are primarily local; other parts are city, or county, or metropolitan; still other parts can best be done at state or national levels. This does not set aside the principle; the complexity affirms it. The complexity suggests the need to recognize interdependence and interrelationships as well as the need for cooperation and communication between levels. It also indicates the need for careful analysis to determine who can do what best.

The complexities also suggest the necessity to recognize primary roles and supporting roles, and the importance of each in the total task of mission. People in the theatre and in the world of sports have learned this better than Christians and Christian churches. Christians and churches tend to be soloists and to play best when they have lead roles. When someone else carries the lead they drop out, or become mere spectators—sometimes critical spectators or Monday morning quarterbacks—rather than supporters. To take the Jersey City case: The lead role was for the churches of Jersey City. The state council had an important "support role" to play in offering counsel and in providing moral backing.

The local congregation which took the initial action also had a support role to play as one of the churches of the city. However, it would be human if both the state council and the local congregation lost interest when they discovered that they could not carry the lead role. It often happens!

In my counseling with councils of churches regarding new structures or new program directions, a principal service has been to help them identify their concerns, and then help them sort out the various levels. Some concerns are best addressed at the local level (for a local council of churches), and other concerns are better handled at a county level, or at the state, or national or world level. Having done this sorting, the council can see its responsibility as a local council more clearly. For those tasks that are best handled at other levels, I have encouraged them to ask, "What responsibility can and should the local council assume in getting things started, and in providing a continuing supporting role?" Also, "What is our part in an on-going task regarding that concern?" In dealing with a state council or a metropolitan council the same questions are asked, only the level of approach is different.

The same identifications can be helpful for local congregations, and for districts or conferences or synods in the denominations.

PROBLEMS AND BARRIERS

What has been said about mission in community seems simple, and clear and logical, yet churches are not operating according to these principles! Why not? Because this calls for new thinking, more knowledge, and different structures, and there is resistance in the churches to all three.

New Thinking

The "think" problem is crucial. Mission in community as described in this chapter is a little complicated and people prefer to think of mission in more simplistic terms. Some are satisfied to read and recite the biblical imperatives. If they look at community at all, they do so in a simpler context, identifying time and place with a local neighborhood within two miles of the brick-and-mortar called our church. Some see mission tasks in world dimensions, but concentrating on the uttermost parts of the earth, they fail to note other tasks at their doorstep or in the metropolis where they live.

A second "think" barrier is related to identification of mission only with those things which the local congregation can do, or which some structured extension of the local congregation can do. Congregationalism supported and was supported by the early 20th century team-haul concept of community which we described earlier and criticized as inadequate to our world. By the same token congregationalism in its extreme forms does not fit our present world. In fact, the realities of the 1970s call upon the "congregationalists" to discover themselves again—not as *the* church—but as parts of the *church.* They must see that only as they band together with other parts can they discover and do what God calls them to do in the neighborhood and beyond it.

Who are the active agents for the church in mission? A third "think" barrier is related to this question. The church is the people of God, and 99 percent of them are lay people. Unfortunately many, including many Protestants, identify the church with its professional army made up of the clergy plus a few employed or otherwise aggressively active lay folk who exercise significant influence on the institution. The clergy and these institutionally-related lay people have their roles to play in mission. But the principal tasks of mission in the world still need to be done by 99 percent who fulfill their vacation and mission of doing God's will primarily through their activities in the secular world—at the sales counter, on the garbage truck, in the court of law, the legislative hall, the hospital, the business office, the farm, the home, the classroom. Only when we catch this vision of a total "people of God" deployed into every area of life, can we begin to hope that God's call to mission can be heard and his church can respond with any degree of competence, propriety or force. The professional army is pretty inadequate for the tasks to which God calls his church, and we need to know that.

Clergy collars may be helpful visible symbols of the church's presence on certain occasions, but thinking, praying, acting Christians in overalls, or nurses' gowns, or judges' robes, or chemists' aprons are the ones who make Christ known, and who discover and do his will in their respective arenas. The church is called to enable and to equip them for their tasks. The laity in their vocations are primary agents in carrying forward God's will in the places where they live and work.

More Knowledge

We said earlier that to discover what God is calling us to be and to do in the human community of time and place we need to know the community as well as the Bible. We have given new dimensions to the concept of community in this chapter and these must be understood as a starting point. However, one must move beyond these basic understandings to more specific knowledge about the community at each of the many different levels in order to understand what God calls us to be and to do. Churches must ever grow in knowledge of communities if they are to serve them, for the specifics of the mission call depends on the realities of the human situation in time and space.

With respect to each community level, we need to know about people and their concerns and problems, about institutions, about issues, about history, and about resources. I shall have more to say about these in the chapter on planning. Admittedly it is not possible to have up-to-date information on all of these matters at every community level. Because of this we can have only partial understanding, and it is well to be aware of this limitation. Even so, we can respond in faith to the light that we have. At the same time we can continue to seek for deeper understanding and more light.

Different Structures

Congregationalism is a part of American church culture. Although the orientation is more pronounced in congregational churches (Baptists, Disciples of Christ, United Church of Christ) there are traces of it in all churches including Episcopal, Orthodox and Roman Catholic. A visiting bishop from the Church of England remarked that as he observed church life in America, all of the churches were congregational. Apparently, this is a part of the American ethos. Congregationalism did fit frontier life well, and it adjusted easily to the town life of early twentieth century. It still serves reasonably well in ministry at the local level. I do not suggest that the congregation be discarded as a basic instrument of mission. It still has an important role to play. Responsibility for mission should be as local as possible and the local congregation can be a primary instrument for mission at the local level. Its mission tasks have been discovered and developed over the years: gathering people into circles of fellowship, preaching, administering the sacraments, teaching, comforting, counseling, marrying, burying. Furthermore, the congregation is in itself a primary community where people are mutually enriched as they experience the family of God relationship. It is also the unit that lifts this experience beyond its own circle into the larger worldwide fellowship of the whole family of God which is the "holy Christian church, the communion of saints."

The trouble is that in most villages or neighborhoods churches do not have structures to enable them to engage in serious exploration of mission together. Nor do they have structures for undertaking tasks that they could and should be doing together. Some communities have them; nearly every community needs one. It would mean not only significant ecumenical advance, but it could also result in significant economies for the churches, and a common witness in the community will elicit better response from the community as a whole. Working together will also add many new dimensions to mission in neighborhoods, for many tasks now go untouched because they cannot be handled by a single congregation.

Such an ecumenical structure need not be complicated. However, it should include more than clergy meeting for lunch, for the clergy are not the church. The insights and involvement of laity are crucial in any such program. A local ecumenical mechanism may be organized as a local council of churches. It may be some kind of cluster parish, neighborhood parish, or larger parish. It can be helpful regarding any issue: schedule arrangement with the public school, drug addiction, joint advertising, law enforcement, joint evangelism, ministry to retired people, chaplaincy scheduling, religion in the public schools, week of prayer for Christian unity, joint Christian education, youth centers, pollution control. The usual leadership training programs might be arranged, summer youth programs scheduled. Some churches join hands to provide an improved bulletin service or a weekly news sheet. Joint use of specialized staff in music, education, counseling, youth leadership, is possible. Surely the structure should provide a means to bear one another's burdens in problems that arise in any one of the churches. It should likewise be a means for common celebration and rejoicing at the progress of any one of the churches.

While local ecumenical structuring is essential, local intra-denominational mechanisms are also needed since a local neighborhood often includes two or more churches of the same communion. Merging two congregations into one merely because they are of the same denomination may not be wise or possible. However, continuing entirely separate units of the same communion in the same neighborhood may not be wise or efficient either.

Thus, even at the local level we have structural problems hampering the up-dating of our congregational thrusts for effective mission in the 70s. When we move beyond the local situation to address the questions of mission in a larger context—the inter-neighborhood complex, the county, the trade area, the metropolis—churches are stymied because they are not structured for such ministries. Congregations, except a few with area-wide or metropolitan orientation, are not structured for this larger community thrust. Inter-congregational mechanisms have been tried but they are still suspect in many quarters. Denominational sub-units—association, diocese, conference, district, presbytery, city society—often take on responsibility at this intermediate level but their churchly status is unsure, again largely because of the inherited congregational bias. In what sense are these units "the church in this place?" No one has defined this. When these units attempt to represent the church at the larger level, congregations challenge their action from the local level, and the national denominational organizations question it from the national level. Even those churches which are supposed to have well defined roles for these middle structures of the church have problems concerning the levels of ministry.

The problem is further complicated because except for the channeling, training, and counseling tasks of the middle-body of the church, the specific mission to the state, or to the metropolis is ambivalent, since few if any of these ministries are denominational in character. There is hardly a Methodist attack on drug addiction, or a Lutheran ministry to public welfare administration, or a Roman Catholic address to poverty, or an Orthodox answer to ecology. There is a Christian word, a Christian view; there can be a Christian force. Only as churches find what God is calling them to be and to do in the metropolis, or in the state, or in the region, as one church of Jesus Christ; and only as they are prepared to respond in that way, can they expect much to happen. Only then can they really say that the church is in mission in these larger community structures.

Councils of churches have provided the principal structural means for making this kind of common thrust potentially possible. I say "potentially possible," for they have never quite realized their potential. The reasons are many:

1. Denominational bodies assumed that they could do these tasks as denominations—at least they wanted to try.

2. While the churchly status of the denominational judicatories, (synod, presbytery, city society) are uncertain, the status of conciliar structures is even more suspect. Somehow it has not occurred to many denominational leaders at the regional level, nor to many conciliar leaders, that a council of churches is nothing more, nor nothing less than "the churches together in that place." As such it may well be, as the Seattle group claims, "the council of the church" in that place.

3. Conciliar leaders have lacked a vision of what they are, or of what they should become, in order to do what they should be doing.

4. The ecumenical agencies at best have included only a portion, usually a minority portion, of Christendom.

5. Even that minority portion tries and usually succeeds in keeping the common expression of "the church in this place" weak; for if it were strong it might threaten the status of those who called it into being. This is sometimes deliberate, at other times sub-conscious or even unconscious.

The concern here is neither with conciliar structures nor with denominational structures except to acknowledge that neither is yet geared to the challenging tasks of providing appropriate structures for the churches to become the church of Jesus Christ in mission at various regional community levels — trade areas, metropolitan areas, states, inter-state complexes.

Many efforts have been made to call the church of Jesus Christ to be in mission in the natural communities. We must try again. For God calls and we must hear and heed this call to mission at every level of community!

Community, U.S.A.

This book is about the U.S.A. as the arena for mission for the church of Jesus Christ. The nation is one important level of community. It is likewise a significant level for church planning and action. While many tasks of mission cannot be done at the national level, other tasks are primarily national. This summary picture may suggest an approach to other levels. It may indicate also some of the realities that need to be considered.

One can offer only a broad-brush picture in a single chapter. Even that is only one man's assessment, based on his perspective and perceptions. But as I see it, this is the U.S.A. in the 1970s.

SIZE AND LOCATION

Fifty states—in North America—between Canada and Mexico—3,000 miles long, 1,500 miles wide—that is the U.S.A. Two states are detached from the central mainland: Alaska, 1,000 miles north, and Hawaii, 3,000 miles west. Puerto Rico, a small but important island territory, is south and east of the mainland. A few smaller island territories are part of the nation. Somewhere in U.S.A. one can find every kind of climate, soil, vegetation, mineral resource.

Total Population, Decennial Population Increase

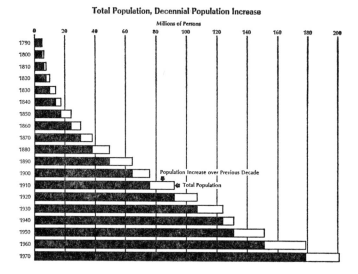

GROWING

Population growth has been continuous since colonial days. In 1789 there was a population of 3,000,000; the 1970 census reports 205,000,000 people. This 1970 figure represents an increase of 11.7 percent over 1960. Growth by decades since 1790 is indicated on bar graph "A."

Demographers estimate continuing growth of 1 percent a year for the next thirty years, and even the most conservative estimates place the population at 270,000,000 by the year 2000.

Most of the time during the 190 years of U.S. history population growth has been regarded as a blessing and a sign of national progress. Now people are questioning whether the country can continue population expansion over a span of years without serious cut-back in its standard of living. The U.S. situation is related to larger questions of world population expansion, and to the problems of pollution and ecological balance. Whatever its implications, the fact to note here is that the nation continues to grow.

ON THE MOVE

Mobility has been one of the unique characteristics of America from the beginning. Indians who first inhabited the land were a nomadic people. The first colonists made what was then an extremely hazardous 3,000 mile journey across the Atlantic to get here. After they came to these shores, the frontier caused them to move again, ever westward.

When the great waves of immigration had ceased and the homestead possibilities were over, other factors stimulated new shifts. Mechanization created a labor surplus on farms, whereas industrialization called for a larger labor force in the cities. World War II, with its specialized call for war workers, accelerated the movement in specific directions. At the height of the war years people were startled to learn that "20 percent of Americans were on the move." When the phrase was explained to mean "20 percent moved each year," people became positively alarmed. The churches too were concerned. A conference of Lutheran churches was held on the theme: "Christ for the Moving Millions" [1] and the Oberlin Conference of the World Council of Churches (1957) devoted one of its twelve sections to a consideration of mobility and its relation to the conference theme: "The Nature of the Unity We Seek."

It is significant to note that the mobility rate of 20 percent a year has remained almost constant since 1945. This means that each year for 25 years, 20 percent of the people in America have changed their addresses at least once! The 1965 story is typical. On the basis of a U.S. census study, during the twelve-month period March

1965 to March 1966, 38,000,000 persons changed their residence address at least once. One third of these, or nearly 13,000,000, moved to a different county, and half of these, or 6,500,000, moved to a different state. On the basis of the 1970 census report the changes of addresses in the twelve-month period of the census was slightly less—only 18.4 percent moved. In 1970, however, the number moving to a different county was slightly higher than in 1965 (almost 37 percent). Among young people, ages 20 to 25, the mobility rate was nearly 50 percent in 1965, and in some years it has been well over 50 percent!

Where do people go? Almost everywhere! They go from farm to city, from city to suburbs. Rural population (farm and towns under 2,500 population not in a metropolitan area) has remained about the same for the past seventy years (between 50,000,000 and 55,000,000). Thus, all the increase in population since 1900 has taken place in cities or in metropolitan areas. In metropolitan areas nearly all of the increase has occurred in the suburbs so that by 1969, 35 percent of the total population of the country lived in suburban rings in metropolitan areas outside metropolitan cities. People move to California and Arizona, to the Great Lakes area, to Texas and Florida, or to the Boston-to-Washington linear city complex.

It should be noted, however, that population flow is not all in one direction. Map "B" opposite makes this abundantly clear. While the data is for the period 1955-1965 the picture is still valid for the pattern of movement is much the same today.

In this shift of population metropolitan areas have experienced phenomenal growth, whereas population in three-fourths of the rural counties in the country has declined, and in two hundred rural counties population declined by 20 percent or more since 1950.

Population Mobility

Interregional Movement

Annual Average (thousands): 1960 to 1965 and 1955 to 1960

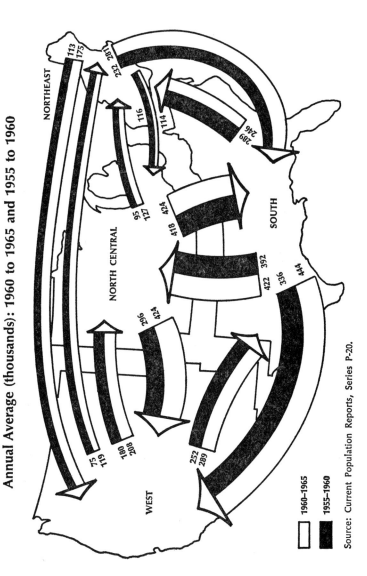

NORTHEAST

113
175

232 281

116

114

289 246

95
127

424

418

424

392

SOUTH

422 336

444

NORTH CENTRAL

296 424

75 119

180 208

252 289

WEST

☐ 1960–1965

■ 1955–1960

Source: Current Population Reports, Series P-20.

AFFLUENT

By almost any standard of comparison the United States is the wealthiest nation in the world. It has the highest Gross National Product (GNP). Its people have the highest level of family income. Americans have more automobiles, more television sets, more refrigerators, more automatic washing machines, more "convenience" household gadgets than any people in the world.

The stewardship of abundance is a major problem for individuals, for nations, for industries, and for social structures. It is a major problem for the U.S.A. Abundance makes the U.S.A. the object of envy of people and nations that have less. If we try to share our abundance we find that it is not easy to do so without patronizing or pauperizing other countries or peoples. Within our country we have a faulty distribution problem. Many have much more than they need. Millions of others live in dire poverty in this land of affluence and plenty.

DEVELOPMENT

American affluence has resulted from a combination of (1) abundant resources, (2) human enterprise, and (3) industrial development. Without the enterprise and resources large-scale industrial development would not have been possible; without the industrial development America would not have reached its present level of affluence. Marketing, banking, transportation, and business management techniques are counted here as part of the industrial development enterprise.

The United States was a nation of farmers at the time of its founding in 1789 with 93 percent of the total working population engaged in farming. By 1965 only 6 percent of the nation's population lived on farms, and many of these were not engaged in farming. Farm residency went down to 5 percent of the total population by 1970. Agricultural production continues to be an important element in the U.S. economy, but it too has become industrialized with much of agricultural production taking place on large farms, highly industrialized and capitalized, and operating on a technical business basis.

Steel, automobiles, aero-space materials, household appliances, military hardware, petroleum, transportation, and home and industrial construction are major non-farm industrial enterprises.

SCIENTIFIC AND TECHNICAL

"If it works it's obsolete" say the technicians at the Cape Kennedy space center! The slogan characterizes the spirit of technological advance in the space program. Other technical areas move at almost the same pace. Three radical scientific developments of the past twenty-five years have made a vivid impression on America: (1) Atomic energy, which brought World War II to an abrupt halt; (2) Jet propulsion which hurls man through space at suerpsonic speeds; (3) Landing on the moon, which was, according to Neil Armstrong, "One small step for man, one giant step for mankind." The space landing became vivid to many of us because we watched its progress in our living rooms through television, another scientific marvel. We may not understand the technical details, but we recognize that these things are possible only because of vast scientific advances. Chemists claim to be on the verge of creating life in a test tube!

Mechanization, enriched by electronic devices and data processing, moved us from the industrial age into the technocratic age, and we do not yet foresee what the future might be. A man's full life story can now be recorded on an inch of tape, and a full print-out of that history can be secured in a minute. Pieces of information

about a given subject can be gathered from 20 parts of
the world, fed into a central computer, recorded, ana-
lyzed, and conclusions drawn from that information elec-
tronically, in less than a minute! What next?

ADVANCE IN KNOWLEDGE

The knowledge explosion is a direct consequence of
scientific and technological advance. Already there is
more to know in every field than anyone can absorb,
and further knowledge grows in geometric proportions.
We need microfilms and electronic tapes to store this
new knowledge, and the librarian of tomorrow will be
the skilled technician who knows which buttons to press
to retrieve the information when it is needed!

Optimists speak of educational advances. More people are in school, and they continue in school longer than
ever before. Very likely students learn more each year
than their parents did. Even so, we are not keeping
pace, for there is so much more to learn. Half of all we
know has been discovered since 1950, and as much more
will be discovered by the end of the 1970s!

URBAN CULTURE

The emergence of metropolis as a social reality is one
of the unique developments of the past half century.
Industrial developments and technology have been contributing factors in this metropolitan movement, but
there are other factors as well. By 1969, 65 percent of
the population of the U.S.A. lived in larger city regions
technically defined as standard metropolitan statistical
areas.[2] The 30 largest metropolitan areas (over 1,000,000
population) listed opposite have a combined population
of 74,000,000 or over one-third of the total population
of the nation. Another 20 standard metropolitan statis-

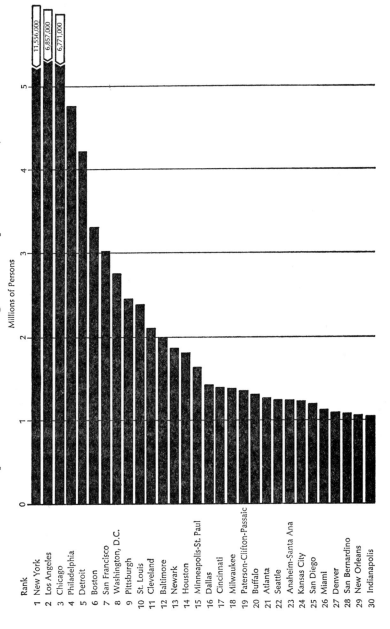

Population of the 30 Largest Metropolitan Areas, 1967

Millions of Persons

Rank		
1	New York	11,556,000
2	Los Angeles	6,857,000
3	Chicago	6,771,000
4	Philadelphia	
5	Detroit	
6	Boston	
7	San Francisco	
8	Washington, D.C.	
9	Pittsburgh	
10	St. Louis	
11	Cleveland	
12	Baltimore	
13	Newark	
14	Houston	
15	Minneapolis-St. Paul	
16	Dallas	
17	Cincinnati	
18	Milwaukee	
19	Paterson-Clifton-Passaic	
20	Buffalo	
21	Atlanta	
22	Seattle	
23	Anaheim-Santa Ana	
24	Kansas City	
25	San Diego	
26	Miami	
27	Denver	
28	San Bernardino	
29	New Orleans	
30	Indianapolis	

tical areas have populations from a half a million to one
million

Urban culture is not, however, limited to these vast
metropolitan areas. It is very much a part of city life
generally across the land, and modern transportation
and communication devices bring 20th century culture to
the remotest corners of the country. Every farm boy can
know the latest rock tunes or baseball scores, and most
of them have seen the Rose Bowl parade on television.
While it is possible to isolate oneself from other people
today, both in country and city, it is also possible for
people in Mountain Valley to be as up-to-date as the
folks in Kansas City. Many city people are, in fact, more
provincial than their country cousins.

LAND OF MANY CULTURES

The urban orientation to our American culture has not
made that culture uniform. Instead, America continues
to be a land of many cultures, imported with the immigrants and modified by the influence of new settings.
Acculturation takes place, to be sure, as each culture
influences, and is influenced by contact with others. Yet
the varieties persist and grow side-by-side. Cultural
pluralism is more apparent and more accepted now than
it was 20 years ago. We have witnessed a number of
significant cultural re-assertions in recent years by Span-
ish people, Black people, and American Indians. These
re-assertions have given Orientals courage to affirm their
distinctive language and value systems. Other recent
immigrants from European countries likewise honor their
traditions. Jewish, Dutch, Italian, Irish, British, Scandi-
navian heritages have been with us for a long time.
With tolerance of differences in our midst subcultures
have emerged within the country. One that has received
much attention in the 1970s is called "youth culture." It

accentuates new life styles and value systems, partly in protest against the systems and values of the older generation.

PERPLEXED WITH POWER

Is ours the most powerful nation in the world? Probably. At least most Americans would like to think so. We did intervene, along with other nations, in two wars and came out as victor on both occasions. We possess stock piles of atomic weapons and vast resources of atomic energy plants as well as more conventional sources of power. We propelled people to the moon, landed them there, and brought them back again three times by early 1971! We possess vast wealth and ours is a great military power. Unfortunately, the nation is uncertain how it should use this power. We desire to use it for the good of mankind, but we are not quite sure what that good is.

UNCERTAIN ABOUT GOALS

Perplexities concerning the use of power are related to a greater uncertainty concerning the direction in which our country is heading, or the direction in which it should be heading. President Eisenhower named a commission to develop "Goals for America," and the commission made its report suggesting a number of clear directions. However, these were not taken seriously, nor has the country settled on other alternatives. Instead, the nation drifts with only limited or interim objectives which a president or a current Congress may identify. People are not called to respond to over-arching national purposes to which they can commit their energies, around which they can rally, and for which they can make sacrifices. The nation seems content to maintain national honor and protect its favored economic position. We are no longer committed to "make the world safe for democracy," "to bring justice to all," "to give equal opportunity to all," or even "to make America beautiful."

UPSET BY RISING EXPECTATIONS

Some groups in America have found group goals for themselves. Instructed and inspired by the best of America's tradition concerning justice and equality they have caught a vision of their right to determine their own destiny and to share in the abundance which others enjoy. The vision has come to those who were among the traditionally dispossessed. It is the substance of various Black movements, Chicano movements and Indian movements in America. It is part of youth rebellion. Those rising expectations call for changes in established social groupings and in relationship systems, and many people are upset. A different dimension of rising expectations, prompted by the new technology, upsets people in other ways because of the tremendous price tag. We had a dream of landing a man on the moon, but it cost us $2,000,000,000! We dream of supersonic air transportation, but that means another $2,000,000,000 for development alone! Decent housing for all means many more billions! Equal educational opportunity for all means more billions! Yet we have grown to expect these things.

RACE TENSIONS

One cannot describe America in the 1970s without referring to the racial tension resulting from the rising expectations of Blacks, Spanish-Americans, and American Indians. It is one of the scars on the U.S. horizon. Indians were here long before white men came, and Spanish-Americans and Blacks were among the first settlers. However, the U.S. early became "white man's country" because European colonists came in great numbers. Indians were driven westward, and Blacks were imported as slaves. Spanish-Americans had their western and southern centers, but they became a numerical factor in more recent times.

The Civil War freed the slaves, but the status of the Black population in the country was definitely second class and servant class for almost another century. Blacks were restricted in housing, handicapped by inadequate educational opportunities, and discriminated against in jobs. While doors did open for a favored few, improvements came slowly and Blacks properly objected to a "gradualism" that kept them from "equality of opportunity" with their white brothers. Dramatic changes have come in the past 20 years. All legal restrictions have been removed regarding jobs, housing, access to public facilities, voting. Blacks have been given leadership roles in churches, in entertainment, in sports, and in many industries. However, discrimination in subtle forms is still with us, and the struggle is not over. Attitudes on both sides tend to keep the 10 percent Black population from participating fully as contributing members with the white majority in building one nation under God.

The same might be said about the Spanish-Americans who also assert themselves as a group to be counted in American life. So too the American Indian.

CONCERNED ABOUT ENVIRONMENTAL POLLUTION

Ecology was a strange word to many people in 1960. By now it is an in term and every magazine in the land carries articles about man's relation to his environment. Alarms have been sounded about pollution of water, air, land, the skyline, the upper atmosphere. Anyone in New York or Los Angeles whose eyes have smarted for three days as a result of atmospheric inversion can understand the reason for alarm. A recent ocean oil spill inspired a dozen major magazine articles. The stench caused by dumping factory or city refuse into a river gives everyone a vivid reminder that man cannot live this way much longer and survive. Most of us are familiar with the junk heaps of discarded automobiles along highways, and we have objected to the miscellaneous debris of beverage cans, scrap paper, and cigarette stubs left by careless tourists. These are everyday pollution matters in which everyone is involved.

Population is another dimension of ecology. When four people live in a square mile of land, natural processes of decay take care of garbage and other disposable wastes without a problem. Increase this number to 40 persons per square mile and the ecological balance changes considerably. Steps must then be taken for a more systematic handling of garbage and wastes. Raise the ratio to 400, or to 4,000, or to 40,000 persons per square mile and the changes become radical—yes even drastic. How many people can be maintained on a square mile? How many people can be maintained in the United States? How many people can be maintained in the world? These are serious questions for today. The four horsemen of the apocalypse—war, famine, pestilence, and disease—provided a crude but cruel natural ecological balance in an earlier day.

However, in this age, when war has become unpopular, and when pestilence and disease have come under scientific control to a large extent, life expectancy in the civilized countries has doubled, and infant mortality has been drastically reduced. This accounts for the rapid rise in population, the concern for ecological imbalance, and the serious discussions about the need for some rational form of population control to balance the present extension of life expectancy.

OPTING OUT OR TURNING OFF

Are the problems of America which we have been describing too heavy to bear? They seem to be for many people, and they provide the rationale and the excuse for people to opt out or turn off from their responsibilities. This is very apparent with respect to political responsibilities, and with all the pressure and promotion related to a national election only half of the eligible voters actually cast their ballot. In many local elections less than 20 percent of eligible voters choose to exercise their privilege. People opt out in other ways too, and the use of drugs is a current illustration. In 1971 drug addiction has received more attention than any other single problem. Presumably, this is because young people have been much affected by the present trend, and because their entire future may be impaired, even by just experimenting with the fad.

While the new drugs receive primary attention, the alcohol problem is still very much with us. Alcoholism is on the increase. The relation of cigarettes to throat and lung cancer is well enough established so that printed warnings are required on cigarette packages, and cigarette advertising is restricted by law.

END OF FRONTIER

Dr. Joseph Sittler, an eminent theologian at the University of Chicago, has suggested that one of the reasons for the rapid accumulation of recognized problems in the U.S.A. at this time is that the country has come to the end of the frontier. He points out that many of the problems have been with us potentially for a long time, but heretofore, we have always had a way of escape by moving on westward, leaving the problem behind. The West Coast is now saturated with people, and we no longer have an escape hatch. Either we stay where we arc and live with our problems, or we return to some place from whence we came to pick up the problem that we intended to leave.

Although the explanation does not cover the whole gamut of problems, this "end of the frontier" is one part of reality in the U.S.A. in the 1970s, and it has very much changed the psychology of the American people.

ONE PART OF SPACE SHIP EARTH

Not only have Americans reached the end of their own frontier, they have also discovered that these United States are a part of one world and a rather small world at that! For the first time in history man has been able to see this world as it appears from the moon, and it looks rather small! The "space ship earth" image, which several writers have developed in recent years, reminds people and nations that they are dependent on each other, and that it is necessary to preserve or to restore ecological balance if we are to continue to live at all. The space ship image illustrates that responsibility, for that balance rests with all of us, just as responsibility for services to that limited space ship rests with all of us.

RELIGION

This book is concerned about the Christian church and its mission in the United States. Chapter 1 gave a cursory picture of religious pluralism, which is characteristic of the churches in America. A little more should be added here.

Religion played an important part in early colonial history. Religious motivations brought a number of important segments of the population to these shores after the country was founded in 1789. The free exercise of religion was guaranteed by the constitution.

At least a majority of the population is formally affiliated with some church in this country, and a "census of religion," taken by the Census Bureau a dozen years ago, indicated that nearly all of those responding expressed a religious preference. Apparently there are not many atheists or agnostics in the U.S.A.

While most of the Christian population is Protestant, the Roman Catholic church with its 35,000,000 members is by far the largest religious body. The Southern Baptist Convention and the United Methodist Church come next, in that order, each with over 10,000,000 members. However there are regional differences. The Roman Catholic church is largely urban, largely metropolitan in fact. The Southern Baptist Convention has its strength in the South and Southeast, and it is by far the largest single body in the South. Lutherans in turn concentrate their strength in Pennsylvania and in the North Central states. The United Methodist Church has the most widely representative distribution in all parts of the country of any church group. Half of the 5,000,000 Jewish members live in the New York Metropolitan Area.

THEREFORE

It has been the purpose of this chapter to describe, rather than to prescribe, in an attempt to develop a thoughtful understanding of this national community as one of the important arenas for mission of the church of Jesus Christ. Answers to major national problems can be found, and under the leadership of God's Holy Spirit the church of Jesus Christ has much to do and much to say to this U.S.A.

CHAPTER 5

Planning for Mission in Community

Let's define planning. It can be:

1. The process of rational decision-making.

2. The process of discovering and defining our goals and devising means for achieving them.

3. The process of determining how to get from here to there, after we know where *there* is.

4. The process of determining a rational ordering of priorities in order that we may also discover appropriate areas for intelligent neglect.

5. The process whereby we relate the principles of the first three chapters and the data of chapter 4 in this book to the practical questions of concerned Christians: "How do we get down to brass tacks?" "How do we put these ideas into action?" "What do we do now?" "How do we go about it?"

6. The process of discovering what God is calling us to be and to do in this place at this time in history, and determining how to go about those tasks in faithfulness to his call.

7. The process whereby we assess the facts, the factors, the forces, and the future of society, in the light of the mission and purposes of the church and of the churches, with a view to accomplishing the mission and achieving the purposes effectively and efficiently.

While the last three definitions apply directly to the concerns of the church and her mission, the first four indicate more precisely what planning is all about, and they highlight important directions for the planning process which need to be considered: rational decision-making; discovering and defining goals; getting from here to there; ordering priorities; intelligent neglect. One might properly pause to reflect on each one of these ideas. The planning process includes all. In practical terms these definitions point us to four questions:

1. What business are we in?

2. Where are we now?

3. Where ought we to be?

4. How do we get there?

Note that each of the definitions describes planning as a process. It is important to understand this emphasis. Because planning is a process, it is ongoing, with neither a beginning point nor an ending point. We often confuse planning with plan making, which is an activity, or with specific plans, which are products. Hopefully, the specific plans are a result of the orderly planning process, but the two are not the same. It is with the process that we are concerned in this chapter.

The last definition is repeated here because it opens the way to engaging in the process to which the other definitions refer. In line with the concerns of this book it is related specifically to church planning: *Church planning is the process whereby we assess the facts, the factors, the forces, and the future of society, in the light of the mission and purposes of the church and of the churches, with a view to accomplishing the mission and achieving the purposes effectively and efficiently.*

Dividing the definition into its four component parts simplifies it a little:

1. The four *F*s (facts, factors, forces, future).

2. Mission and purpose.

3. Accomplish and achieve.

4. Effectively and efficiently.

THE FOUR *F*s

Chapter 4 introduced some of the facts, factors and forces concerning one level of community—the national community, U.S.A. It hinted also concerning aspects of the future. One dare not confuse planning with fact-finding, but planning must begin with the facts about the community level with which it is concerned. The facts must be discovered and communicated, and they must be respected, even though facts may not always support preconceived preferences and prejudices.

Facts

1. We must know about people:
   a) Who lives in the community?
   b) How many people live there?
   c) What are their racial and ethnic backgrounds?
   d) What are their ages?
   e) What are their family patterns?
   f) What are the family or individual incomes?
   g) What is the educational level, and the educational spread?
   h) What are the cultural patterns?
   i) What is the rate of mobility?
   j) How do they feel about the church? about the community where they live?

2. We need to know about the community, and the

church must ask its own questions of the secular culture and its institutions:

a) What are its natural boundaries?
b) What is its relation to the larger regional community of which it is a part?
c) What are the natural smaller communities within the community level studied?
d) What is its history?
e) Does it have economic stability?
f) Is the community fragmented or cohesive?
g) What is the rate of delinquency in it?
h) What governmental structure (or structures) operate in serving the community?
i) What are the voluntary community organizations?
j) What are the transportation facilities?
k) What are its health and welfare sources?
l) What are its other service resources?
m) Does it have a good school system?
n) What kinds of power structures are operating in it?
o) How do decisions get made, and why?
p) When decisions are made, who gets hurt?
q) Who cares about the community? Who cares for the community.
r) Where is the pain? Who hurts? Why?

3. We need to know about churches. (Depending on the level of concern the questions may primarily relate to congregations, or judicatories or national denominations).[1]

a) How many are there?
b) Which denominations are represented?
c) What is the membership of each church?
d) What kind of facilities do the churches have for service?
e) What are the "people" resources for leadership (both lay and clerical)?
f) How do the churches relate to each other?

    g) What church history is relevant to this community?

    h) What are the churches doing in the community?

    i) What can the churches do that no one else can do in the community?

    j) What kind of worship, education, and service programs do they offer?

    k) What do the church people identify as concerns and issues for the church and the community?

    l) How many people in the community are without church affiliation?

A bit overwhelming? This is only the beginning! Planning is complicated enough even if the facts alone were all that had to be taken into account. Unfortunately, there is more—much more! Many good plans, based on the logic of the facts, have not produced constructive results because less tangible factors and forces in the social situation were not taken into account. These factors and forces are just as real as the most objective statistical data, and often more important. Since they do not lend themselves to charts and tables they are often ignored or dismissed. We do so at great peril!

Factors and Forces

1. *Theology.* Theology brings God into the planning picture. God is a "factor" and a "force" and must be dealt with theologically and actually in planning. To complicate matters for the planner, however, there are theological differences. These differences complicate the planning task but they do not absolve the churches from responsibility for planning, nor do the differences suggest that churches cannot plan together. In the light of the premises and affirmations of Chapter 1 regarding "one church of Jesus Christ in all the world," theology rather compels us to plan together, for in spite of our differences the church is really one, and churches which claim

to be a part of the church are really only different members, but members of one body. Imagine the chaos in your body if the different members did not plan and work together!

2. *People.* Planning would be much simpler if we did not have to take people into account. But they are here, and it is really for people that the church is concerned. Those who work in urban redevelopment admit that people who must be relocated in order to clear land present one of the most knotty problems for them. Urban planners have learned to accept the problem. We of the church, proclaiming the sacredness of human personality, ought to be just as ready to accept people. Some are stubborn; most are selfish; many are short-sighted; more are uninformed; a few are terribly unreasonable. Yet here they are, and our principal concern is for them. To complicate the picture even more, we not only plan *for* people, but in this day of participatory democracy we have also learned that we must plan *with* them.

3. *Prejudices and Sentiments.* Much as we hate to admit it, most people are motivated more by their prejudices and sentiments than they are by the facts of life, or even by the call of God! Church planning cannot surrender to prejudice, nor can its conclusions be based on sentiment. On the other hand, the planner must take these factors into account. Overcoming them often becomes a central planning problem, as anyone knows who has tried to lead a congregation to pursue an inclusive membership policy, or to relocate a church building away from the cemetery grounds!

4. *Irrationality.* Since planning is supposed to be a rational decision-making, those who engage in it always encounter frustration because it must take people into

account and, as has been said in the previous paragraphs, people do not make their choices and decisions by rational processes. Planning, therefore, needs to develop a rational approach to human irrationality. While it can never achieve total rationality, the process can lead toward making rational decisions.

5. *Social Experience.* Social experience of people is an important planning consideration. Some have had rich and positive experience in working together; others scarcely know one another. If people have had little contact with one another, planning may need to begin at the very elementary level of getting people to talk together. A negative experience in trying to consolidate schools, or trying to coordinate garbage collection, will greatly affect how people respond to proposals for adjustment or cooperation between individual congregations.

6. *Culture and Cultural Patterns.* Those creations of man's hand and mind and heart to which he attaches value constitute his culture. This culture is so much a part of a person that to say we must reckon with him means that we must also take his culture into account. It determines his prejudices; it molds his sentiments; it provides the background for much of his social experience. The relation of the church and its mission to contemporary culture is too large a subject to deal with here. We call attention to culture as a genuine factor that must be recognized and considered. For a full discussion of the subject we suggest Dr. Richard Niebuhr's *Christ and Culture.*[2]

7. *Social Trends.* Nothing is so powerful as an idea whose time has arrived! These powerful, contemporary social ideas manifest themselves in the social trends in communities and in society at large. Church planning evaluates these trends, encourages positive directions,

and seeks to arrest or re-direct unwholesome tendencies. Social trends sometimes provide the supporting force, at other times they pose the chief obstacle for the planner. Trends are always factors with which planning must reckon.

8. *Organization.* Church planning must recognize social and political structures as well as church structures. Admittedly, many of the present structures are obsolete and need overhauling. However, planning need not wait for these organizational changes. We can work with what we have, and develop means for planning with and through present structures. Planning often becomes the mechanism through which we identify the need for new structures or for changes in old ones. Structures are only means toward an end. If the means are not adequate, they need to be changed. This need for change should become evident through the planning process.

9. *Power Structures.* Power structures are sometimes identical with social structures or church structures, but not always. For planning one must know who has authority in civil society to enforce laws, to improve highways, to provide welfare and similar services. One must also know and reckon with the less formal but highly important industrial, financial, labor, civic, social, and personal power structure in communities at different levels. These less formal structures are sometimes less obvious, and they need to be discovered and related to the planning process.

Consider the personal power structure, as an example. In almost every community there is some person or group of persons to whom the community looks to give the affirmative or the negative nod. He may be the banker, or the mayor, or a leading elder in the congregation. He may be much less visible. The communication experts describe him as the "legitimizer." Soil conserva-

tion people call him "Sam," and when they work in a
community they immediately try to discover who Sam
is in the community. He is a power person, and either
an asset or a serious obstacle for the planner. In my first
parish the legitimizer was a widow who held no official
position in the congregation. With a little thought the
reader can readily identify the legitimizers in the community level in which he is interested and concerned.

10. *Resources.* Financial and leadership resources must
be carefully reviewed. It is to no good purpose to propose
vast plans for new congregations, or church facilities,
or social services if there is no possibility that financial
resources can be secured or that leadership can be
secured and trained to put these facilities to good use.
Because of the resources factor, finance and personnel
become important elements in the design for action
phase of the planning process.

11. *Change.* Change is one of the constant factors
with which planning must reckon. The new element in
our day is that the rate of change has been greatly accelerated. Facts change from month to month. So do
sentiments, prejudices, social experiences, cultural patterns, and economic possibilities. The rapid rate of
change requires that planning be dynamic and flexible.
It is necessary to keep abreast of change, to anticipate
its directions, and to keep the planning process moving
and adjusted to the changes that come every day.
Change makes the process element of planning extremely
important.

This discussion of factors and forces is by no means
exhaustive. Let it be clearly understood that planning
is not captive to them. But they must be reckoned with
and assessed. Then a major focus of planning may be to
resist or to re-direct, or overcome, or encourage, or guide,
or stimulate one of these factors or forces.

FUTURE

Planning must take the past and present into account; yet its focus is on the future. Sometimes planning will take the long look to 1980 or to the year 2000; at other times it takes a more immediate look to next year, or to the next five years. Both the immediate and the longer range look are important components of the planning process. Without the long range vision the immediate will lack focus and direction; without attention to the more immediate the long range look becomes dreaming rather than planning. Planning means making decisions about today's problems in the light of tomorrow, and is related to goals which we seek to achieve at some more distant future.

Unfortunately, we see through a glass darkly. The surprises of the past 30 years convince most of us that we cannot be sure about tomorrow. Demographers in 1930 who forecasted a static population in the United States by 1960 are the first to admit this. A single invention, or a single misdirected atom bomb, could throw off every intelligent prediction. Researchers are now working on a pill to control coronary defects, and if successful it could move life expectancy to 120 years! Think what that would mean—55 years of retirement after 65! Admitting the propriety of caution regarding the future, we still look ahead, and we make probable prognoses. We also plan probable directions and appropriate possible alternatives. Our decisions will not always be right, but if we act with intelligence we can be just as right as the business executives who also must make major decisions today in anticipation of the possibilities and the uncertainties of tomorrow.

Change in the Future. Surprises in the future? Yes! But change in the future will not be one of the surprises for churches that plan. Rather it is one of the purposes of church planning to determine what to change, and why, and how, and then to plan in order to affect the necessary changes, in line with the church's understanding of her mission and purposes. Dr. Robert Hoover, a professor of planning, has defined planning as "the process of rational change." Church planning not only seeks to adapt the church to the future, whatever the future might be, but it actively seeks to make that future as God would have it to be. Another person has defined planning as "the process of inventing the future." Church planning is concerned about that.

Not everything should be changed. Church planning is not committed to change for the sake of change; some changes need to be resisted, and some old things need to be conserved. However, *metanoia,* one of the New Testament call-words, is usually translated "repent" or "repentance," and this means "turning about," "turning back," "change of mind," "a change of direction." Status quo is not implied in repentance; the word calls for radical change! The writer of the Book of Acts reports that when Christians came to Philippi the citizens exclaimed, "These men who have turned the world upside down have come here too" (Acts 17:6). To engage in church planning is to look for, to expect, and to find ways to effect change in people, in institutions, in society.

MISSION AND PURPOSE; ACCOMPLISH AND ACHIEVE; EFFECTIVELY AND EFFICIENTLY

The planning process brings the insights gained from research into the four *F*s together in sharply focused planning questions:

1. Now therefore, what specifically is God calling his church and his churches to be and to do in *this* community of time and place? This is the mission

and purpose question. It is the goals question, informed by the nature of the church, the revelation of Scripture, and the social setting.

2. How do we go about the task (or tasks) in order to accomplish what we are to do? This is the implementation question. It is concerned about accomplishing and achieving mission.

3. How do you go about doing so effectively and efficiently?

These questions are included in the process. Details for effective and efficient operations are outlined in the two chapters that follow. However, it is important to understand the process. A brief outline is included here.

PLANNING PROCESS DESCRIBED

While the planning process does not quite fit scheme or schedule, I outline eight simple planning steps in dealing with any problem:

1. Definition of the problem

2. Survey

3. Analysis

4. Goal and policy formation

5. Design for action

6. Viable alternatives

7. Implementation

8. Evaluation, feedback, and review

The outline is helpful as a means of analysis and description. The planner is the first to admit that planning does not flow from point to point as easily as the outline might suggest. At the same time he cautions that we should not jump from survey to design for action without analysis and policy formation. Viable alternatives must be considered as one develops the design for action. The planner emphasizes the importance of feedback and review which will start the process anew, leading to better policies and improved design for action. Some prefer to place the steps of the process in a circle to make clear that planning does not stop with step eight. Evaluation, feedback, and review close the loop and start a new planning cycle; after this cycle comes another, and another, and so on. That is the nature of planning as process.

A few explanatory observations may be helpful concerning each step.

Defining the problem at the beginning is very important. It is also very difficult. Much planning is fuzzy because the problem is not clear in the minds of those who plan, or, planning may be irrelevant because having been hasty in defining the problem, the planning group did not get at the real problem. It is helpful to reduce the statement of the problem to a single sentence or question. Explanatory or descriptive paragraphs may be added if they are necessary.

Survey. With a clear definition of the problem, planning proceeds to gather the facts and to identify the factors and forces that bear on that particular problem. We call this survey. This may require formal research. It is concerned with what we know, and what we need to find out about the problem.

Analysis. Planning then proceeds to analyze these facts as well as the pertinent factors and forces to answer the question, "What does this mean?" in relation to the stated problem. Already at this stage of the process one may discover that the problem is not correctly defined, or that more information is needed before one can hope to find answers. Thus, as stated earlier, the schematic outline does not accurately describe the process; already at step three the planning group is re-checking steps one and two.

Goal and Policy Formation. One definition of planning reads: "Discovering and defining our goals and devising means for achieving them." Defining the problem, survey, and analysis should point first of all to what we are supposed to be doing—toward a goal.

Before further discussion, we must define how four terms are being used. All four are used in speaking of future expectations and devising ways to reach or achieve them. But each of these terms carries a specific connotation.

1. *Aims* are very general directions often incorporated in a statement of purpose. More indefinite aims may be the assumed purposes. The aim of the congregation may be to grow, or to serve the community, or to preach the gospel. The aim of a council of churches may be to promote Christian unity, or to help congregations work together.

2. *Goal* is an end state or condition to be reached at a given time in the future—five years, ten years, twenty years. Goals are usually stated in measurable terms, though not always. They indicate where we wish to arrive or how much we expect to achieve by a certain time.

3. An *objective* is a more immediate yearly or monthly achievement as a step to be taken to reach the goal. If the membership of a church is 300 in 1972 and the goal is 500 by 1980 the 200 increase could be divided into eight equal parts, and the objective for 1973 would then be 325 members.

4. A *policy* is a determined general direction. Policies usually determine goals. Thus, before a council of churches can have a chaplaincy goal it must have established a

policy beforehand: that it would carry on a chaplaincy ministry. Before a council can have a goal regarding a rent-subsidy housing project, it needs to adopt a policy regarding that kind of sponsorship

There are operational policies as well, which determine how goals may be accomplished. Thus, some congregations have a membership policy that encourages church membership only from persons who live within a two-mile radius of the church. Such a policy would control how a congregation set about to build its membership to 500 in the next eight years.

Design for Action. Having established where we are going, we ask, "How do we get from where we are to where we want to go?" The question sets forth a new kinds of planning problem, and the planners go back to steps 2 and 3 of the planning outline with this question as a new problem. The concern is to develop a design for action.

Viable Alternatives. There are always several possible courses of action. This is an assumption of planning. Presumably one of the alternatives is better than others, and the planning task at this point is one of appraisal. However, before we make choices, we deliberately seek to discover various possibilities. We ask: "In the light of the facts, what will likely happen if we proceed as we have been?" "What will likely happen if we change to course 'A'? to course 'B'? to course 'C'? What are other possible directions we might take?" Most people do not take enough time to discover the different alternatives, and the possibilities of each. They rather select one that looks attractive and spend their time selling this course of action to their fellows. Thus, they cease to be planners making rational decisions, and become salesmen instead.

Elements of a Design for Action. Almost every design for action requires a communication schedule for information and interpretation; it may require a promotional activity as well. Funding, personnel needs and training, new organizational patterns, and priorities become necessary parts of the design. One surely must set up an order of events and with this a tentative schedule to make the design realistic. Reduced to writing, this table of events and time schedule become a PERT (Progress Evaluation Review Technique) chart, and it is a real aid to the person who must administer the design. This will be described in more detail in the next chapter.

In the design for action we must know what the design is intended to accomplish. Technical planners use a five point schedule: 1) concept, 2) feasibility, 3) development, 4) controlled field testing, and 5) full implementation. They tell us that most major industrial developments pass through all five stages, that each of the last four calls for a design for action, and that each calls for a different design. This helps us clarify what we are designing to do.

Implementation. Moving from design to action is termed implementation. This means getting the job done. We are concerned about that, for we plan in order to accomplish the mission and achieve the purposes of the church effectively and efficiently. Without implementation, planning is only picture drawing, or perhaps only dreaming! While church planning and social planning can never be quite as exact as an architect's drawing, it must be practical enough and detailed enough so that one can move from design to action. Implementation is really administration, and we will deal with that in the next chapter. We mention it here because the implementation phase must be in mind as a part of planning with a practical concern for planning that can be put into action.

Evaluation, Feedback, and Review. I will deal with the *why* and *how* of evaluation in more detail in the

closing chapter. I introduce the subject here to emphasize that evaluation is an integral part of the planning
process, usually starting the planning circle over again
with new or revised problems. Furthermore, it is necessary to emphasize that an evaluation system should be
built into every design for action. Evaluation cannot be
an after-thought. It should be included as an integral
part of any adequately planned action program. More
than that, it needs to go behind these action programs to
challenge the policies, the goals, and the objectives on
which the designs have been built, for these too need
to be reviewed. Evaluation calls for careful and challenging review. Feedback suggests the action which
places this reviewed and evaluated experience back into
the planning process for the next cycle.

STRUCTURES FOR PLANNING

The basic planning structure of any agency is the
central decision-making body of that agency as described in its constitution and by-laws. For most congregations the planning body is its session or vestry or
church council. For most councils of churches it is the
board of directors or the executive board. Communions
and subdivisions have their corresponding decision-making boards. Planning is decision-making, related to establishing policies and goals and setting priorities, and that
is the responsibility of the central boards. Program boards
or committees, in turn, have central planning responsibilities within their assigned areas.

A number of structural principles are listed below
which should help boards and agencies carry out their
planning functions:

1. *Authority.* Those responsible for execution of plans
must be involved in the planning process. If they desig-

nate representatives, then those who are so appointed must have authority to *represent* the responsible person. This does not mean that the detailed work of gathering or analyzing and communicating material cannot be assigned to staff persons or to subcommittees. It does mean that the appraisals of data, the policy review, and the designs for action must be selected by those who have authority to execute the plans which they develop and approve. A clear implication of the planning definitions is that planning is an executive function, to be undertaken by those persons or those boards who have authority to make the decisions.

2. *Continuity.* Planning is a process. It follows that planning is not accomplished from 9:00 to 4:00 on a particular Thursday. It is important for boards with decision-making responsibility and for executives who organize board agendas to realize this. Each meeting may address itself to a different facet of the problem, but there should be continuity from one meeting to the next, and this continuity must be realized and clarified.

Continuity is necessary also in personnel. To have six people present at one session and six others, just as competent, at the next session, means that little or no progress has been made. Good minutes help provide continuity for persons who must be absent, and proxies may sit in to report back to the members who must be absent, but continuity of personnel is important to real planning progress.

3. *Handleable Units.* Some planning is handicapped because the planning unit is too small; planning is likewise hindered when the unit is too large. The size of units that can be handled, in turn, depends on the nature of the planning problem. For some problems a four block region is large enough; for others an entire metropolitan region or a socio-economic region like Southern Appa-

lachia is necessary. The regional concept, as well as the levels of community principle described in Chapter 3, suggest possible appropriate units for planning. A region has been defined as that unit which provides the most appropriate context for decision-making concerning an identified problem. The important point to note here is that the unit should be large enough so that the problem can be comprehensive; it should be small enough so that it can be handled. If the unit is too large it can usually be broken into smaller parts, and the parts handled one at a time.

4. *Timing and the Time Factor.* Planning takes time, and this is part of the problem. People are usually more willing to invest money in planning than they are to devote the necessary time to it. Yet we can hardly be faithful in mission unless we take the time to discover what we are supposed to do, and how to do it. Properly understood and properly undertaken, planning saves both time and money. At least business thinks so, and most business enterprises require careful planning, even for apparently minor matters like committee meetings.

Timing is another aspect of the time factor. Nothing is so powerful as an idea whose time has arrived! There are dozens of illustrations of this principle in history, in scientific development, and in our own personal experience. The patent office reports that it often receives patent applications for identical items from widely scattered parts of the country within the same week; apparently the time has arrived. An important educational technique is to teach children when they are ready for it, or to develop readiness for a new idea. This is also a necessity in social planning, and in church planning. If people are not ready for a new idea or a new approach, we may need to wait, or we may need to move more slowly, or we may need to include readiness training as part of the design for action. On the other hand we may discover that the church is already behind the times, and we may have to run to catch up or to keep up. Planning moves most easily when timing is appropriate to the social situation.

5. *Group Process.* Church planning is usually group planning. Therefore, structures for planning should include the group factor. The principles and techniques of good group process cannot possibly be outlined in a few paragraphs. Suffice it to say that group process involves inter-personal relations, and it is sometimes difficult to move at a rational level when emotions come into play. The skillful planner can do much, however, to overcome emotional barriers by developing and maintaining positive attitudes in the group: to himself; to others in the group; to the concept of change; to the problem itself; and to the process through which the group must move. The attitude of the leader in these matters plays an important part in setting the emotional tone for others, though it does not always determine their attitude, since other factors also come into play.

Experts tell us that where group decisions are required, and where group relations break down, it may be necessary to forget the planning problem temporarily in order to resolve the inter-personal conflicts or negative feelings before making any real decisions.

6. *Communication.* "Planning is communication." Although this is an apparent over-statement, it emphasizes the great importance of communication in decision-making and in implementation. When communication breaks down within groups, or between groups, or between individuals, then planning breaks down too. Thus the planner must develop and perfect his skills in communication. To do so he can learn to use simple communication tools such as charts, graphs, displays, tables, color

slides, the printed page, the telephone, as well as the more complicated tools of group process public speaking, or others. Members of the family of God cannot make rational decisions for God's kingdom work unless they can communicate with one another in the process of making those decisions.

7. *Specialized Roles.* While the executive or the appropriate executive board must make the decisions, we have indicated that they can make use of persons with special skills as helpers in reaching decisions and in carrying forward projects on the basis of these decisions. Learning how to use such persons with special skills represents major growth on the part of a leader at any level. The usual helper roles in planning include research, analysis, interpretation, communication, goal and policy formation, evaluation. Sometimes a consultant from the outside can help by bringing an objective perspective and by proposing alternatives on the basis of his wider knowledge and experience related to the problem, or on the basis of contacts and observations he has made from other areas.

IN CONCLUSION

Church planning is not easy, but I believe that it is about the only way to faithful response to God's call to mission. Churches plan in order to accomplish the mission and achieve the purposes effectively and efficiently. The mission and purposes are God's. Churches need to learn what God is calling them to be and to do in this world, in this time, in this place. They need to learn how to proceed to do that work in response to his will. They are concerned to be faithful. Effectiveness and efficiency are aspects of this concern.

CHAPTER 6

From Planning to Action

"Plan the work; work the plan; then take a second look." This describes the task of almost anyone who has leadership responsibility. The chairman of the anniversary celebration committee of a local congregation sees his work in these terms. The phrase outlines the leadership tasks of a parish pastor, or of a council of churches executive, or the head of one of the national boards of a denomination.

Planning, administration, and evaluation—the tasks are interrelated, yet they are also separate and distinct. While anyone in leadership identifies with all three, some are more involved with one than with the others. To accomplish the mission and to achieve the purposes of the church effectively and efficiently the leader must be knowledgeable concerning all three.

ADMINISTRATION MEANS PUTTING PLAN INTO ACTION

Administration means getting the job done. It means doing what one decides should be done according to approved plans. It means making the necessary adjustment decisions that must be made in the process of implementing the plan in order to reach the desired objective.

We mentioned the *PERT* chart in a previous chapter. The *PERT* system was developed by the United States Navy as an administrative device. The name is an acronym meaning *Progress, Evaluation, Review Technique*. Developing such a chart is a planning discipline. Once developed, it provides the action outline for the administrator. When it has been carefully prepared, the administrator has his guide, including the order in which things should be done. The administrator works the plan. Without his skill and service the most careful planning comes to nothing.

We insert a simple *PERT* chart here for three reasons: 1) to illustrate how a chart might be set up; 2) to show a planned sequence order of events, and 3) to illustrate how the plan becomes a guide to the administrator. This particular chart is related to the May appeal letter for Luther College in New Jersey, where I am a member of the Board of Regents. This chart is a very simple one, dealing with one simple action. Charts for more complex activities become complicated indeed! Some readers may have seen the PERT chart for a space flight in which activities are listed in terms of minutes and seconds!

The value of the chart as a guide to the administrator and to his supervising role in relation to others is quite apparent. It outlines the plan of operation and indicates who should do what, and when it should be done.

Unfortunately, everything does not happen according to plan! Disruptions may be caused by simple things like the breakdown of a mimeograph, or a letter that failed to arrive. Plans may be upset by a mail strike, sickness, or a resignation. A major crisis developed in my experience just ten days before the beginning of a national conference in 1970 when one of the principal speakers was unable to fulfill his commitment. A replacement needed to be secured on short notice. It became the

PERT Chart for May Appeal Letter

Action	Date	Acting Body	Action Person	Supervision
Decision to issue letter	Oct. 12	Fin. Comm. Board of Regents	Development Director	Development Director
Format and design approved	Jan. 14	Fin. Comm.	"	"
Writer assigned task	"	"		"
Order for supply and stamps	Jan. 18		Business Office	"
Draft letter prepared for review	Feb. 22		Pub. Rel. Officer	"
Draft letter circulated for review	Feb. 24-March 4	Draft Comm.	Treasurer	"
Check on supplies and stamps	March 4		Dir. of Devel.	
Letter finalized	March 10	Fin. Comm.	Pub. Rel. Officer	"
Processing of letter, addressing envelopes	March 14-March 25		Business Office	"
Mailings: Third class	April 8		"	"
First class	April 15		"	"
Assemble data concerning responses	Daily		"	"
First report	June 14	Ex. Comm.	Treasurer	"
Continue to assemble response data	Daily		Business Office	"
Final report, analysis, evaluation	Aug. 12	Fin. Comm. Ex. Comm.	Treasurer	"

task of the administrator, and whatever supporting committee he had, to make the adjustment decisions that were necessary so that the conference could be held in spite of the upset. These adjustment decisions become the business of the administrator.

ADMINISTRATION MEANS WORKING WITHIN THE ADMINISTRATIVE TRIANGLE

Whenever authority is assigned or assumed, and accepted, an equal and corresponding responsibility must be assigned or assumed and accepted. Vice versa, whenever responsibility is assigned or assumed, and accepted, an equal and corresponding authority must be assigned or assumed, and accepted. With authority-responsibility assigned or assumed, and accepted, provision must be made for channels of accountability by those who assign and by those who accept, and proper accounting should be expected and insisted upon by both sides.

This is the administrative triangle. It is important in successful administration. Violate it at any point and someone gets hurt. Work progress slows down as well. Yet the principle is ignored every day!

Consider the plight of the faithful secretary. As the executive hurries out of his office to attend a two-day meeting in another city, he instructs her to "get these letters in the mail by Thursday." He returns to find the envelopes, stuffed and neatly piled on the table, but not mailed. When he asks for an explanation (a simple instance of accountability) the secretary replies: "I did not have authority to buy stamps, and we did not have them on hand!" Of course she might have assumed the authority, but she had tried that two months earlier in a similar situation and was reprimanded at that time for exceeding her authority.

The executive sometimes gets into a similar bind. A major issue develops in the city council concerning a controversial summer recreation program. The council executive is consulted; he expresses his judgment, even though the council has had no occasion to discuss the question. He does not report the matter to his executive committee when it meets. A week after the executive committee meeting, his judgments are quoted in the press. His executive committee calls him to task. In the emergency situation, he assumed authority. However, he neglected to utilize an opportunity for accountability. The committee was quite within its rights to call him to task, and he had to accept full responsibility for the authority he had assumed.

Illustrations could be multiplied. Often there is a lack of balance between authority and responsibility. Accountability is important, and often ignored. Staff members do not give proper accounting to supervisors or directing boards and committees; committees do not give proper accounting to general boards or assemblies; general boards or assemblies give poor accounting to supporting judicatories or congregations. Then they wonder why people lose interest. Often the channels for accountability are unclear or even closed. If so they must be clarified and they must be opened. Without accountability people shrug off responsibility, and often they either assume too much authority or none at all!

Whether one supervises or is supervised; whether one is part of a planning committee or board, or task force, one needs to ask: "What responsibilities do we give (or have)?" "What authority must we give (or have)?" "To whom are we accountable?" If responsibility, authority, and accountability are clear and appropriately assigned, staff members and boards and committees can function efficiently and effectively.

ADMINISTRATION MEANS WORKING WITH PEOPLE

Rarely is administration a solo operation. If plans are outlined carefully and no major interventions hinder, moving plan to action is still not routine because it means working with people. They are both bane and blessing to the administrator, but people are never routine. They are the prime "stuff" through whom the administrator works and for whom he works. It is of crucial importance that he see them as people, not things or categories. People are uniquely different from anything else with which the administrator works. I assume that leaders with a concern for the church in mission will have at least the basic Christian orientation concerning the unique place of people in God's world: created in God's image; little lower than the angels; sinners, yes, but still the object of God's love and of his redemption; destined for eternity. This is true of all men: the reader, his boss, his colleagues, his staff, his helpers, his clients, even his opposition. This kind of basic Christian understanding of man should help the administrator answer three basic questions of our world: "Who am I?" "Who is my neighbor?" "What is my relation to my neighbor?" Secular business counselors emphasize the importance of recognizing the individual in business relations. Even more in church administration we should both assume and affirm the importance of persons.

You Are a Person. "Know thyself," is a first require-
ment of an administrator. Know yourself as a person and
know where you fit in the scheme of things. Know your
special abilities, your limitations, your individual hang-
ups. Sensitivity training is often a part of training for
administration, and it is included to help administrators
discover themselves as human beings. The administrator
is a person, not just like anyone else, but not too different
either! Administration begins with you—you are a person,
with all the dignity, the needs, the problems, the aspirations, the limitations which that term implies.

You Work with a Boss. Everyone does. If you are top
man in your organization the boss may be a board, or
even a constituency, but in any case there are people or
groups to whom you are responsible and accountable,
and he or they have certain authority over you. If you
are not the top man, the boss is easily identified. Many
administrative breakdowns occur because the administrator has not learned to relate positively to the person
or board to whom he is responsible and accountable in
the operational system. It is important to accept the
facts about these relationships; then to understand them;
then to respond positively to them as a relationship of
people to people. The boss, with his faults and his assets,
is a person too.

You Work with Peers. They are people with position
and responsibilities similar to yours in your organization or in different organizations in the work of the
church. The pastor of a neighboring church is a peer
to a local parish pastor; the executive of the Baptist State
Convention is peer to the Lutheran synod president;
heads of two parallel departments in a national board
are peers. Here again, positive relations are important.
No single unit can do the work of the kingdom. With
positive relations each can support and aid the other.
With negative relations each hinders the other. This

should be obvious, it is not always so! Workers in the church waste a lot of energy because of personal stresses that develop between peers. It happens at the level of congregations, at the level of councils of churches, as well as at national denominational levels. The cause? Pride, jealousy, pettiness, lack of inner security, lack of vision on the part of one or both persons.

The remedy? Recognize other individuals as people. Your peers are people too! Recognize also that you have common tasks as colleagues in kingdom building. Recognize the need for other tasks than yours; if the kingdom is to grow, acknowledge the need for the contribution of others in that work.

You Work with Staff. Every task in the contemporary church is a team task and the effectiveness of an administrator is very much determined by the way he builds and works with his team. The team may be synonymous with staff; at least the staff becomes the core of the team. Staff members are usually thought of as paid workers; in church work the staff members are often faithful volunteers: teachers in the church school of a local congregation; committee leaders in a local council of churches.

Whether paid or volunteer, the administrator has nine responsibilities in relation to his staff: 1) describe the job; 2) select; 3) support; 4) train; 5) supervise; 6) counsel; 7) evaluate; 8) correct 9) discipline.

1. *Describe the Job.* A person must know what the job is before he can select a person to fill it, and any person invited to undertake a task has reason to ask, "What do you expect me to do?" If the administrator can describe the task and the expectations precisely, he will know the kind of person he should seek and the training and special qualifications required. The person sought, on the other hand, will understand the task which

he is asked to do, and he can know whether he will be interested and challenged and able to undertake it. Writing a job description for a committee chairman may seem tedious, but it can be very important to the chairman and to the administrator. Written job descriptions for paid staff are essential for effective administration.

2. *Select.* Once a job has been described the administrator's task is to select the right man or woman to do the task. Get the right person for the job and a task is half accomplished! Careless selection means continuing administrative problems.

3. *Support.* The right person for the job deserves adequate support. If the task is a vocational one, this means salary and other allowances. These should be adequate. Whether paid or volunteer, support includes space to work, tools to work with, other necessary equipment. Support includes attention from the administrator. The kinds of support should be clear when a person is asked to undertake a task. One hesitates to ask qualified workers to invest their time and talent trying to make bricks without straw. If it must be so, prospective staff should know the situation when they are asked.

One support which every person deserves and requires is a sense of personal worth and personal accomplishment. For many people this is more important than salary, security, or status. It becomes a primary motivation for that host of volunteers who make the work of the church go forward. The administrator should be aware of this personal need, and he should point out the areas of possible service and accomplishment to the prospective staff person. When a staff member undertakes a task, the administrator should help him find this kind of fulfillment by giving encouragement, by recognizing work well done, and by expressing appreciation for faithful service in the face of discouragement and obstacles. Development is a second need for most people. A prospective staff person should be told how he may grow in an assigned task and how the administrator and the organization he represents is willing to help in that growth. This may include continuing education or special training provisions. The challenge to growth for teachers is one of the unique features of the Bethel Bible Study series, (Adult Christian Education Foundation, Madison, Wisconsin) and it captures the loyalty and time of hundreds.

4. *Training* is a particular aspect of support. Even though a person may be well qualified for a task it does not follow that he or she knows all that is needed. At least the staff member will need orientation. The administrator has the responsibility for allowing time and providing the necessary assistance. Training may be needed to develop special skills. Work arrangements should make provision for continuing education to help staff grow with the task. It adds to job satisfaction, and through staff growth the work goes forward.

5. *Supervise.* Every staff should expect and should ask for supervision. The eagle-eye, watch-dog type of supervision was never very effective, and fortunately the method is now passé. However, intelligent oversight by the administrator provides real support to the entire staff, and more work is accomplished. Accountability of staff to the supervisor is one aspect of supervision. Staff should be prepared to give this accounting; they should welcome the opportunity, and the administrator must give attention to it.

6. *Counsel.* Every staff person should know that he or she may turn to someone to check out ideas or to talk over personal or professional problems. This counseling role belongs to the administrator, and the more skilled

he is in it, the better he serves his staff, and in turn the better they serve the work.

7. *Evaluate.* Every staff person should welcome an appraisal after three or six months of service, and at least annually thereafter. Each worker wants to know the answers to questions like: "How am I doing?" "Am I making progress?" "What should I do better?" "What am I doing wrong?" Evaluation sessions need not be formal, though an annual formal evaluation session with the supervisor is a welcome experience. It should include recognition of progress and achievement as well as discussion of problems and deficiencies. It should afford an opportunity to talk things over with respect to obstacles as well as future plans and directions.

8. *Correct.* The evaluation session may be used for correction, but staff members appreciate correction whenever the administrator senses the need for it. To know that the administrator will correct promptly when he sees the need for correction gives staff members a sense of security. Because staff people are human beings, they know that they make mistakes and they need correction. Usually it is better to ask them to make the correction rather than the administrator doing it himself. Never let corrections become a matter of personal conflict between the administrator and a staff member!

9. *Discipline.* If the administrator has followed the suggested order through the first eight steps, discipline will not be required often. However, discipline is a part of staff administration and it is sometimes necessary even in the best situations. Prompt disciplinary action, before problems become chronic, is more effective than delayed action. On the other hand, precipitous action is often resented. Timing is important in discipline; so is fairness. The respect for the person as a person must be a consideration.

You Build a Staff Team. An administrator might follow all nine principles of staff administration just listed, and still the work may not make significant progress. These are person-to-person principles, indicating ways of dealing with individuals. Individuals are important. However, most tasks are accomplished only when these individuals relate themselves to one another as members of a team.

The primary role of the administrator is to develop this staff team. He is leader of that team with special responsibilities, but every other member is important also and each has a special role to play. These roles are related to one another as parts of a total task. Each member needs to see the total picture, and each needs to see how his or her work contributes to the whole. Each member should see the contribution of others as well. In the team approach the administrator emphasizes goals, purposes, and the team. Staff members are not so much working for the administrator as they are working with him or her and with other members to achieve the goal. The administrator calls the plays and oversees the process, but he does so in the leadership role of a team operation. Modern business calls this the *purpose* approach as contrasted with the *bureaucratic* approach.

Clerical staff are a part of that staff team. How could one get anything done if letters were not typed, or envelopes filled and stamped and delivered to the mail box? Clerical staff need to see how their work contributes to the whole. This builds morale. More than that it builds people, for when people see a purpose in what they are doing, they grow. Fortunately too, more work gets done, for people work better and faster when they sense the meaning and worth of their work.

You Work with Volunteers and Special Workers. These staffing principles and relationships apply whether the administrator works with paid or with volunteer staff. They apply whether people work full time or part time. Administrative sensitivities are even more important in working with volunteers or part time staff since the opportunity for continuing contact with them is more limited, and the administrator does not have the same leverage with them as with salaried staff. However, having been a part of volunteer staff teams, and having observed others in action, I know that many of these have worked as hard, and as long, and as faithfully as paid staff. This has been true when the administrator observed positive staff principles in working with them.

Many ministries in the church are served by volunteer workers who do special tasks, sometimes single tasks, in relation to on-going programs. Some of these are specialists—musicians, artists, lawyers ,accountants, writers. Others may do general and even routine tasks—fold bulletins, stuff envelopes, mow the lawn, shovel snow, arrange coffee breaks. These persons are special staff and they have a staff relationship to the administrator. Their work is important. Staff principles are valid in relation to these too, even though application of the principles may not be as apparent. These workers are people too. They need to see meaning in the things they do. They need support; they may need training. They appreciate attention; they deserve counsel. If they are not doing their tasks adequately they expect correction. We take them for granted at great peril to ourselves and to the work of the church.

You Work with a Supporting Constituency. No administrator can ignore his supporting constituency. He who tries risks death for the work! Supporting constituency are people too with the same drives and the same limitations that others have. Usually the supporting constituencies in church programs are not unreasonable, but many of them are uninformed. If they feel that they are being ignored by the administrator, or that they have not been involved in what he is doing, the gap between the administrator and the supporting constituency widens quickly and support is threatened. At least the constituency wants to be informed. If they can be involved in some way in determining directions or in carrying forward the tasks, the gap betwen administration and supporting constituency closes quickly and support is secure.

Pronouns are the key. So long as the supporting constituency identifies with the program by describing it in terms of "we" and "our" and the administrator identifies in the same way with the constituency, support will be assured. Change the pronouns so that the supporters refer to the program as "your" or "they" or "it," and the administrator refers to the supporters as "they" and to the program as "mine," and support slips rapidly. Relations with supporting constituency are as simple as that, and just as sensitive.

You Work with Clients. A client is anyone who receives service; therefore, there are clients in the mission and ministry of the church, for the church is called to serve! Who are the clients? Congregations? Members of congregations? Surely one kind of ministry must be addressed to them. Many think that the primary ministry of a congregation is "to serve those who belong to it and pay the bills." *I prefer to think of members of the congregation as the force, rather than the field!* Then it is the business of the congregation, as a corporate body, to gather, to train and to marshall that force to undertake mission in the world. In the same way local congregations are the force which a local council of churches gathers, trains, and marshalls for work in the larger community of the city or the county. If the congregations see themselves as the field and the council as the agency to serve them, then this needs to be clarified!

Who are the clients? Whom are we called to serve? The questions are pertinent and need to be clarified before the administrator proceeds very far. The answer determines the nature of his task.

The church is called to go into all the world. In the context of these chapters it is called to go into all of the U.S.A. It has a ministry to all people. Let the administrator recognize that clients are persons—human beings like himself. They need to be served as persons! Whether the people are rich or poor, rulers or refugees, respected or outcasts, the church ministers to them as *persons*. The implications for the style of ministry should be obvious.

The command to go into all the world means that the church also has a mission to the structures of society, for they are critical parts of the modern world. The structures are less personal to be sure, and it may be one of the church's primary tasks to humanize them. We cannot deal with them in the same way we deal with people. Yet people make up these structures, and only people can change them. Thus, even in dealing with the structures of society we are dealing with people—folks, much like ourselves.

You Work with the Opposition. Administration would be simpler and a lot more pleasant if we were dealing only with friends who agreed with us. However, that is not the case, and it is fortunate that it is not so. A major role of the administrator is to deal with the opposition and to recognize the value of the challenge and the creative tension which the opposition brings to the administrative process. A few simple suggestions will have to suffice for this chapter:

1) Respect the person who opposes;

2) Recognize that he renders a significant service by challenging you and the direction of your leadership;

3) Listen to him. He may be right; he may be partly right. At least he represents a different perspective and this is important. Perhaps he is interpreting misunderstandings concerning your work which your friends are too polite to mention or too blind to detect.

4) Try to understand his point of view, even though you do not agree with it.

5) If his position seems at all plausible and if it might involve policy change, bring his position before your board. Let the opposition make the presentation if you can arrange it.

6) Keep the discussion on the level of issues rather than personalities.

7) Learn from him. Incorporate what you can of his insights. Ultimately he may become one of your allies.

8) Having done this, hold your position until you are convinced that his is the better way.

The opposition cannot always be dealt with according to these suggestions. The opposition may not be rational. When he appears as "a roaring lion seeking whom he may devour," we may need more vigorous and forthright response tactics. In kingdom work we are under orders from above, and we are not allowed to compromise those orders simply to get along with the opposition. We need courage to hold our ground in the face of deadly opposition, and the church of Christ often encounters that kind. To hold our ground may mean a cross. It meant just that for our Lord. It meant a cross for many faithful followers whom we honor.

You Work with Major Boards and Committees. The administrator relates primarily to his executive board and to its administrative committee if the board has one. For the church school superintendent this means the church school board; for a council of churches executive it means his executive board or board of directors; for a general church president this means the executive council or the church council.

In this Administrator-Board Relationship, what is the administrator's role? What is the board role? The administrator:

1) prepares for meetings (dates, arrangements, notices);

2) develops the agenda (usually in consultation with the board chairman);

3) assembles necessary materials;

4) reports concerning progress and problems since the preceding meeting, including the administrative actions taken on the basis of decisions made at a previous meeting (this is his accountability);

5) identifies issues requiring action by the board and makes recommendations concerning those actions;

6) arranges when the meeting is over for processing and mailing the minutes, for carrying forward the actions taken, including necessary communication and interpretation;

7) keeps the board informed of significant developments between meetings.

The primary roles of the board are: 1) to establish goals, policies, and priorities; 2) to assign authority and responsibility; and 3) to provide for accountability and support.

The board sets goals, policies, priorities; it also provides the necessary support, including finances, to make sure that things can be done. The administrator carries out the decisions of the board. The distinctions are important both for the board and for the administrator. If the goal of the congregation is 500 members by 1980, the policy of "inclusive membership" has been set, and an objective has been approved to have at least one minority-race person in a leadership role in the congregation by 1975, then it is up to the administrator and his staff to work out how these things can be done and to work at the task until it has been accomplished. If people in the congregation object to the activity of staff in accomplishing these objectives and working towards this goal in line with policy, then the blame and responsibility rest not with staff but with the board. Staff is only carrying out orders. If the administrator wants implementing suggestions from the board, he is free to ask for counsel. It is his administrative task primarily to work out the implementing details and to keep the board informed about what he and the staff are doing.

In relation to the administrator the board serves as: 1) a brake; 2) a whip; 3) a sounding board; 4) a counselor; 5) a supervisor; 6) a buffer; and 7) a bulwark of support. The administrator sometimes needs a brake to slow him down; at other times he needs a whip to speed him up. The board serves both needs! Often the administrator needs a sounding board; sometimes he needs counsel as well. "When in doubt ask the board" is intelligent advice to any administrator. The board expects the administrator to report concerning his work and it receives that report as an accounting of his stewardship. When trouble arises, the board becomes the buffer to share with the administrator the responsibility for unpopular actions which the administrator takes in carrying forward the policies and decisions of the board. When the going gets tough for the administrator, the board becomes his bulwark of support to back him up.

You Work with Departments and Committees. Every organization has sub-committees or related departments. Most organizations have too many. I counseled with one Lutheran Synod that had 23 different sub-committees. Each department or sub-committee needs purposes, goals, objectives, and priorities in line with its assigned responsibilities. Each committee requires staff service by someone. In small organizations the staffing of these special departments and committees is a volunteer service, often provided by the chairman of the committee. In organizations with paid staff, each staff person is assigned to give staff service to one or more of these departments or committees. A general administrator may serve committees directly related to the executive board. The board-staff relationship principles described earlier apply to these departments and committees as well.

You Work with Other Church Organizations. A church organization concerned with the mission of the church of Jesus Christ which does not relate to other church organizations either rejects or ignores the essential premise of this book, stated in Chapter 1: "There is one church of Jesus Christ in all the world." There are many churches; there are many church organizations; there is only one church. The many organizations need to relate to each other as parts of one church. The executive as administrator plays a key role in cultivating these interrelationships.

Church administration means relating to groups in secular society as well, for the church has a ministry to institutions and structures of society: to call them to become God's instruments in the world to promote and to achieve equity, justice, and peace, and to serve the needs of people so that people may enjoy a richer and fuller life.

ADMINISTRATION MEANS COMMUNICATION

Good communication is essential. Without communication there is no administration; poor communication means poor administration. A breakdown at only one point can stop the entire action process, or it can completely change the course. Just one mis-sent letter can

do that! One misunderstood instruction can do the same!
In moving from plan to action we need to learn to tell
it straight and tell it promptly.

The Audience. The administrator communicates with
all the persons and groups listed in the preceding sections: the boss, colleagues, staff, boards, committees,
constituencies, clients, social structures, the opposition.
He also has a word for many public groups beyond his
organization.

Content and Purpose. Communication usually answers
the questions: who? what? when? where? why? how?
It does so to give information, instructions, authorization,
interpretation, promotion, or inspiration. The same message often serves different purposes for different audiences. Thus a set of instructions to the staff may be for
the information of the boss, or the board.

Media for communication are manifold: spoken word,
memoranda, letters, telephone, reports, charts, graphs,
pictures, posters, slides, movies, minutes, articles, addresses, round table discussions, retreats, or these in
various combinations. We could go on and on. *The medium is the message* over-states the case, but the medium
is much more an integral part of the message than most
people realize.

Style suggests the way we use the media. It may be
formal, informal, literary, poetic, simple, or scholarly.
The audience determines the style and an understanding
of the audience level is crucial in determining the choice
of style and vocabulary.

When the administrator knows what he wants to say
to a given audience, he selects the medium which adequately conveys the message, he determines the style
to be followed, and then proceeds to get the word out.
If time is a factor, he may use the telephone or send a
telegram. If time is less important, a letter may serve
better because more can be said, and the written word is

available for review and for filing. When one needs to reach a thousand or more, film strips, tapes, or the printed page may be needed. The same material often calls for different treatment with different audiences. Thus the Missionary Education Movement developed its mission themes for a given year with different kinds of texts addressed to different age levels. Denominational church school boards do the same. Administrators may need to do this also. Instructions to staff may be too detailed and too technical to inform and cultivate the interest of the board or the supporting constituency. Yet, as instructions go to staff, both board and constituency may need to be informed, but in different words and style. If the project has general interest, word also needs to reach the wider public, but this too calls for a still different treatment. I have found a five level classification helpful in planning communication: 1) staff, 2) board, 3) wider interest circle, 4) church constituency, 5) general public.

Listening. Two or more persons are involved in communication: the communicator and the audience. Communication has not been completed when something has been said or written or diagrammed; it is not complete until the message has been received and perceived by the audience. What is communicated is not what the communicator had in mind to say or write, but what the audience received and perceived. The two are not necessarily the same! In this connection it should be said that every good communicator needs to be an attentive listener as well. Communication goes two ways, and he who will not listen will usually not be heard. Surely the administrator needs to be sensitive to the words and sounds and gestures of the people with whom he works, and he must try to understand what they are trying to say by their words and sounds and actions. Communication is hearing as well as telling!

ADMINISTRATION MEANS BUDGET
AND FINANCE

It takes dollars to get things done. Money is an important element in every business, including church business. Christian churches in the U.S.A. raise and spend many billions of dollars every year. According to the 1969 *Yearbook of American Churches* 62 different Protestant bodies had a total spending budget of more than $3,600,000,000 in 1967, and this represented only half of American Christendom! Giving to religion in 1969, according to the 1971 *Yearbook of American Churches*, was $7,930,000,000 or 45.2 percent of all voluntary giving in the U.S.A.

Administration must be concerned with all phases of the money cycle: raising money, budgeting, budget adjustments, spending and accounting, audit, reserves, investments, credit. I can make only brief comments and suggestions here concerning these subjects, and I do this only to indicate that money questions must remain in the purvue of the practical administrator at all times.

1. *Building a Budget.* We begin here because building a budget is the money side of planning. A properly constructed annual budget is a simple and valid shorthand description in dollar symbols of the goals, the objectives, and the priorities of the church agency for the budget year.

Building a budget, therefore, begins with reviewing goals, setting annual objectives and priorities, and then assigning price tags to the objectives and to the activities related to those objectives, based on a proper priority rating of the objectives and the activities. The price tags indicate priorities, even though the administrator and the policy body may not have consciously established them.

Unfortunately most budgets are not developed on that kind of a goals-objective-priority basis. Furthermore, budgets are usually written by accountants to accommodate simple accounting procedures, rather than by program and communication people, and the dollar symbols do not tell the story as they should. On the following page is a sample budget for a local council of churches that should satisfy the accounting people, who work primarily with column A. At the same time it tells the objective and priority story for the council as a whole and for council staff in the program columns.

Budget building means working with three budgets: the one for the current year, the one for next year, and the budget for two years hence. All three must be in the purview of the administrator and in the mind of the budget and finance committee members. This section is written with the assumption that budgets are planned at least two years in advance, reviewed and finalized a year later, and open to modification during the operating year.

From the budget sample it should be clear that priorities in this particular case are on general administration and migrant work: most of the money is assigned in these categories. It is likewise clear that the council office and its staff devote their primary attention to general administration and to research and planning. If, in the column under social concerns, the salary and allowance figures were $10,000 rather than $2,000, this would clearly indicate a different set of priorities for the staff.

People have sometimes asked how one arrives at the figures in the different program lines for salary and office, since checks for salaries and rents are not made out on this basis. These are intelligent advance estimates made by the administrator and his staff regarding their time distribution. In this budget it means that over a third of the time is spent for general administration, and about one-fourth for research and planning. Taken seriously,

BUDGET 1972

	A TOTAL	B General Administration	C Research Planning	D Migrant	E Christian Education	F Social Concern
INCOME						
Congregations	$ 33,000					
Individuals	10,000					
Business & Foundations	2,000					
Church Women United	4,000		1,000	4,000	1,000	
Sales	400					
Registrations	1,500					
Earnings & Services	1,500					
Miscellaneous	400					
TOTALS	$ 52,800		$ 1,000	$ 4,000	$ 1,000	
DISBURSEMENTS						
Salaries & Allowances	$ 30,600	$ 13,000	$ 8,000	$ 4,600	$ 3,000	$ 2,000
Executives (2)						
Secretaries (2)						
Housing, pensions, insurance, training						
Office	4,200	1,700	900	600	600	400
Rent 2,000						
Postage & Supplies 700						
Printing 600						
Telephone 500						
Equipment 400						
Travel	2,500	1,000	600	600	200	100
Meetings	1,600	500	200	200	100	600
Committee expenses	900	300	100	100	100	300
Special program services	9,000			6,000	3,000	
TOTALS	$ 48,800	$ 16,500	$ 9,800	$ 12,100	$ 7,000	$ 3,400
Contingency #	4,000					
FINAL TOTALS	$ 52,800					

To be distributed where needed in revision of budget in September 1971, used for new work, or transferred to reserves

the assigning of figures in this kind of a chart sets policy and priorities for the staff.

The special program service in the budget suggests a possible summer migrant program with employed summer staff, and perhaps a week-day released-time-program or a strong vacation church school program in Christian education.

This is not an ideal budget. When 33 percent of the budget goes for administration—keeping the shop going —there is something wrong and that needs to be discovered. Even so, the sample budget tells a better story than the one from which it was originally developed, for in that budget all but a $9,000 special program services was identified under administration.

Note the explanation concerning the contingency item. Presumably this budget was prepared in 1970 for the year 1972. The budget may be finally revised in the fall of 1971 for administrative purposes and then this $4,000 item will be absorbed in other program lines according to need, or it will be in new program. Any balance will be set aside for reserves.

2. *Administering the Budget.* The budget is a shorthand description in dollar symbols of the objectives and priorities for the budget year. It is also a basic financial policy statement. It is important that the administrator take it seriously and operate the program with the bud-

---

These objectives for 1972 were presented with the budget:

1. Cooperative planning for all phases of mission thrust in the county.
2. Ministry to migrants in all areas of the county.
3. Released time program for all children in the first three grades in school.
4. Develop program for half-way house to serve released prisoners, supported by the county community.
5. Initiate plans for Faith and Order dialogue in the county.
6. Enlist into active membership 75% of the churches in the county.

get as his policy guide. This calls for a bookkeeping system in line with the income and disbursement items of the budget. Within the approved budget framework the administrator is expected to operate without further reference to the board. If the entire printing allowance has been used up during the first six months of the year this means that there can be no more printing during the rest of the year unless there has been underspending in some other budget line. In that case the budget amounts can be changed by action of the proper board. This is a policy change and it calls for policy action. Sometimes action is taken authorizing the administrator to change items within the total budget simply by reporting the changes to the board. This authority should not be assumed without proper authorization, and the administrator should exercise the authority with care. It is important for him and for his board to recognize that the budget is a firm policy guide. On the other hand, the budget is not a law—it is a guide that should be followed in spending and accounting, and departed from only where authorization has been made.

Adjusting the Budget. A budget proposed two years in advance should be revised and finalized a few months before it is put into effect. The contingency figure is then absorbed or designated for reserves. During the operating year other adjustments may need to be made within the budget lines (I have indicated ways in which this can be done). Still other adjustments may become necessary because anticipated income does not measure up to expectations, because emergency needs arise that call for changing priorities within the year, or because of emergencies that require additional resources beyond the budget. This becomes a policy question for the board to decide. A very common practice when more funds are needed is to launch an appeal. If reserves are available, it may be wiser to draw on them for quick response to the crisis and then replenish the reserves on a more deliberate basis.

Raising money. Christian churches represent the major voluntary operation in the U.S.A. They are a multi-billion dollar-a-year enterprise, and most of these billions are raised by voluntary contributions. To be sure, there have been suggestions and schedules and major promotional efforts, but even so, the support is still volunteered in the last analysis. The reader has probably been related to raising this money through a stewardship team in a congregation, a finance team in a council of churches, or a benevolence committee in a denomination. Administrators usually have responsibilities for raising money as well as spending it. If they are spared that responsibility, they must keep in close touch with those who have that task, for how we spend money often determines what we receive from the supporting constituency.

This section began with budget building. The goals-objectives-priorities approach was encouraged and related to advance budgeting—at least two years in advance. This kind of advance planning, based on what the church is all about and what tasks it can undertake this year and next, has much to do with raising money. At least it confronts Christians with tasks and ways of achieving them. The stewardship possibilities of Christian churches have been only half-touched because those in responsibility have not helped Christians to discover the challenging tasks to which God calls them. Budgets have not seemed exciting because they have not been presented as dollar responses to divine imperatives. In today's relatively affluent America the churches can afford to do almost anything they decide they ought to do. I have seen congregations and councils of churches double their budgets within two years because they caught a vision of tasks and responsibilities to which God called them.

Budgets with clear objectives and with designated priorities, developed with this kind of orientation, can challenge Christians to get on board with dollars in serious proportions. People are not much interested in emergency appeals to cover the deficit or to help keep the doors open. They are interested in responding to divine imperatives which they hear and see as tasks which they are called to do!

Reserves. Some people regard reserves as instruments of the devil in church business. They may be. However, while spending in church operations is usually on a regular basis, nearly all church agencies experience the summer slump, and many agencies receive half of their income during the last two months of the year. Because of these factors, reserves are necessary or the agencies will need to operate on a credit basis and pay the consequent interest costs. It has been suggested that a reserve fund should equal at least one-half the annual budget to provide a safe cushion for councils of churches, synods, or national church bodies. Local congregations may need less. Some agencies have much more.

Reserves make it possible to operate on a cash basis. They also provide a cushion in case of temporary recession or in case of call for emergency action. When reserves are used in either of these ways, plans should be developed immediately to restore the reserve level.

Credit is a part of finance in today's world. While careless credit produces untold hardship, wise use of credit can double the working resources of the church! Churches have built senior citizens housing, rent subsidy housing, college dormitories, church offices, and most of the church buildings through credit financing. Good credit is almost as important as reserves and in some ways can serve the same purpose. Operating on credit rather than with current cash is more expensive because of interest charges, but wise use of credit is an essential element of financial administration.

The administrator will need to know much more about money than has been suggested here. He will need to understand balance sheets, learn the purpose of audits, reckon with capital gains and losses, consider the possibility of annuities, and so on.

Someone once asked, "When is a business man not a business man?" The answer was supposed to be "when he's a vestryman." In this chapter, I have affirmed that business is very much a part of church administration and that wise handling of money is a very important element of achieving the church's mission. The good vestryman needs to be a good business man in the Lord's business!

CHAPTER 7

Review and Evaluation

We plan for the church in mission; we move from plan to action; then we review both plans and action to determine whether we are going where we planned to go, how well we are progressing, and how we can do better. We ask again, "Is this where we really ought to go and what we really ought to be doing?"

Evaluation is the word which describes this third aspect of leadership. It is as important as planning or administration and is an integral part of both.

ASSUMPTIONS

The evaluation process implies criticism and judgment concerning what the leader has planned and what has been planned and done by others. It assumes: 1) that everything is open to question; 2) that no plan is perfect; 3) that the very best plans for 1971 may be obsolete by 1972 because of new machinery, new data, or a new social situation; 4) that every operational program can be improved; 5) that experience should help us discover and develop better ways of doing things.

Admittedly, this is not the mind-set of many leaders. When they have set a direction and made their decisions, they do not want them to be challenged or changed.

They assume some kind of holy sanction for what has been decided. One needs to grow up at the leadership level to accept the contribution that evaluation can make to the leader and to his program. Boards and committees need to grow up as well, for often the leader who sees the benefits of evaluation is held back by members of his board or committee who object to questioning things that have been decided. "We never did it this way before" is often considered a sufficient closing argument against any suggestion for change.

A NECESSITY

Churchmen and church boards are perhaps more hesitant than others to accept evaluation as an appropriate part of church planning and church administration. After all, they say, churches take their directions from above, and these directions should not be subject to a radical secular approach that questions everything. Some contend that evaluation belongs to God and it is presumptuous for us to try!

We agree with the earnest and the pious that ultimate evaluation in church work belongs to God. However, this does not make the evaluation process inappropriate in addressing more immediate goals and tasks in the work of the church. In fact, our concern for *ultimate evaluation* challenges us to continuing evaluation at deeper levels to make certain that our work and our will and our way are in line with God's way. We want the Lord's commendation, "Well done thou good and faithful servant," but we can hardly expect that commendation if we have not been faithful in little things. These include using the tools and techniques that are available to us to improve and advance his work. Planning is one; administration is another; evaluation is necessary for either of the others to be effective.

Related to Goals

Evaluation is possible only in relation to established goals and objectives, and one of the first benefits of the evaluation process is that it demands that we set clear goals and objectives. Where are we going? What do we expect to accomplish this year? If this has been determined, then at the end of the year we can check whether we have accomplished what we have set out to do. Perhaps we have accomplished only half of it; or perhaps we did more than was expected! If goals and objectives have not been established, there can be no basis for measurement except subjective hopes. These are different for different people, and they shift with changing moods. Without clear goals and objectives almost any program can look good, or look bad, depending on the different expectations of people. Set an objective—120 students, $50,000 income, bi-racial participation in every committee, 100 questionnaire replies received—and there is a basis for measurement. If at the end of the year these objectives have not been reached, and they may not be, we can properly ask why: were the objectives unrealistic? was there a breakdown in communication? a change in the economy? inadequate preparation or training? If the objectives were realized or exceeded we can have the satisfaction of measuring up to expectations! These annual or quarterly objectives should be related to longer-range goals and they should be steps along the way to realizing or accomplishing these longer-range goals.

Evaluation not only checks whether objectives have been realized, but also asks: was it done efficiently? did it take too much time or money or personnel? Evaluation also challenges the objectives and the goals by asking: are they relevant to the basic tasks and purposes to which the church is committed, and are they important enough so that in relation to limited time and money and other tasks that should be done, these tasks deserve the priority they have received?

Build Evaluation into the Plan

Evaluation should be considered in the early stages of planning so that it can give sharp focus to the plans that are developed. The plan itself should provide for adequate review at reasonable intervals along the way of its execution. Unless evaluation is planned in from the beginning, it becomes an imposed extra which people tend to postpone, or to ignore as irrelevant. Unless it is included in the plan, the evaluation idea is resented as outside interference and a lot of extra work for nothing.

By the People Responsible for Planning and Execution

Evaluation by an outsider, whether a firm or an individual, is rarely fruitful regardless of how expert the outsider may be. On the other hand evaluation without outside help is usually inadequate because people find it difficult to be objective. The best evaluation takes place when it can be done by those responsible for planning and execution, but with someone not directly related to the operation present to ask questions, to offer suggestions, to share information, and to point to gaps or blind spots that those involved in the program might not see.

The conclusions and appraisals, however, are not so much made by the outsider as they are the discovered consensus of those intimately involved in the program. When the conclusions are their own, people are more likely to do something about them. A helper need not be an expert in the field; he must be a sensitive listener and a good questioner.

MODELS

Any kind of questioning that will prompt persons to look at themselves and their work critically can serve for purposes of evaluation. I offer two models that I have found helpful. With slight modifications either one can be used in the evaluation of an entire program of a congregation or a council of churches or a national church body. Either one may be used in relation to a specific agency or a specific committee program.

Model A

This model has the advantage that it can be reduced to a chart and a check sheet (see opposite page). In using the chart a rating system of 1 to 5 is followed, assuming that number one is the very best and number five the poorest, with number three as a median quality number. If no rating is possible in a column the space is marked with an (X); if the particular item is not pertinent a dash (−) is placed in the appropriate space. In line with the suggestions in the previous section, I have found it valuable for the responsible people in the opreation to do the rating. However, it is also worthwhile for the outsider to have a rating sheet so that he can make entries concerning his own personal appraisal. These may then be compared in a summary session with the ratings of those who were involved in the program.

Columns A, B, and C deal with purposes, goals, and annual objectives. The principles behind these inquiries have been stated earlier. Evaluation begins here because many leaders in congregations and in councils of churches have only vague notions as to why their organizations exist. Even if constitutions or other official charters designate purposes, they may have been forgotten. When leaders do verbalize purposes, their stated purposes often

	A	B	C	D Efficiency			E Effectiveness		F Relevance					G	H
				a	b	c	a	b	a	b	c	d	e		
	Are annual objectives clear?	Are goals clearly stated?	Are purposes clear?	Is activity commensurate with cost?	Does activity require heavy overhead of time and money?	Does activity involve clients to help?	Does activity move toward goal?	Does activity achieve objective?	Is activity accepted politically?	To what extent is it used?	Does it fulfill established policy?	Does it perform an assigned role?	Is role itself relevant?	Are there objectives for coming year?	Has activity been given a priority rating?
Name of Department or Agency															
Name of Person Reporting															
Name of Evaluator															
Major Program General															
1.															
2.															
3.															
4.															
5.															

(Use rating scale in each column 1, 2, 3, 4, 5, with "1" representing the best) Use this space for comments regarding any program have little relation to the established official purposes. Some national communions and their judicatories do not fare much better. In an inquiry concerning the official stated purposes of a dozen communions made some years ago I learned that many of the statements had not been revised in the last fifty years and most of them were thoroughly inadequate for the church in today's world. Fortunately, the practices of the denominations were far better than their stated purposes! Hopefully, the constitutions have been up-dated concerning purposes since then.

If purposes are vague, goals will also be hazy. Even when purposes seem clear many agencies fail to identify goals in line with these purposes for the next three, or five or ten years. Ask their leaders and they insist that they are too busy to clarify what they intend to achieve by their efforts. Yearly objectives related to these goals are hardly considered pertinent.

Often the first round in an evaluation process gets no farther than columns A, B, and C. If an organization gets a rating of 4 in column A, 5 in column B, and an X in column C because there are no annual objectives, then the rest of the chart becomes irrelevant. Even so, significant evaluation has taken place, for it becomes quite apparent to the evaluator (hopefully one intimately involved in the program) that purposes, goals and objectives must be clarified before intelligent progress and further evaluation can be expected.

Provision is made in the first line under columns A, B, and C to rate the unit as a whole in terms of its purposes, goals, and objectives. In the lines that follow, major program elements are listed and purposes, goals, and objectives for each of these must be rated.

Sections D, E, and F are related to major program elements. They deal with efficiency, effectiveness, and relevance. Efficiency is concerned with getting the job done at little relative cost. How much do we get for our dollar? Do those who receive the service share in its cost or in the work load? We need to check efficiency. However, not everything that is efficient is effective, and no matter how efficient an operation may be, it does not rate well unless it moves the agency toward achieving objectives. On the other hand, sometimes one needs to sacrifice efficiency to achieve effectiveness. Then again, some programs are so inefficient that we cannot afford them even though goals and objectives would be accomplished if these programs could be done. Column *a* under E is concerned with moving toward goal; column *b* with reaching objectives.

What difference does it make? That is the concern of the relevance criterion. Does the work have some degree of public acceptance? Is the service used? To what extent does the service fulfill some established policy? Does it perform some established role of the organization? Is the role itself relevant to the needs of the church, or of people and society in our day?

Suppose a denominational health and welfare board set up a mobile health unit for use in Appalachia. The intentions of the board were no doubt good. However, if the community rejected the mobile health unit, and if only two persons came for service each day during the first year, the relevance on those counts would rate pretty low. Even so, the mobile unit might rate well in the next columns: it fulfilled an established policy of the board, it is a program in line with the role of the organization, and very likely the people in Appalachia needed that kind of health service. A low rating on two counts does not necessarily mean that the program should be discontinued. It does suggest that the approach may need to be changed.

Columns G and H look to the future. Annual objectives are very important and in this ever-changing world a program that claims first priority in 1971 may rank only third in priority in 1972, and by 1973 it may deserve no more than a rating of 5 or 6. At least we should not take for granted that because a youth camp has received 40 percent of the youth activity budget for the past four years, this ratio should continue indefinitely. Perhaps new kinds of ministry to youth will be more important than youth camps by 1973. A priority review and a priority rating each year indicates a more intelligent approach to mission. Priority ranking calls for evaluation, and it means making choices on the basis of that evaluation. This may mean that some good things will need to be left out in favor of other things that are more important in today's world. Then, so be it!

Model B

To some readers model A seems too formal and too much like business. It is business—church business! They may prefer model B. It is evaluation in four dimensions, and it is based on Paul's letter to the Ephesians where he speaks of "length, breadth, depth, and height" (Ephesians 3:18).

1) *Length* is the statistical dimension. It asks how much, and how many? How many worship services were held? How many worshipers attended? How many calls were made? How many patients were served? How many dollars were gathered? How much was given for benevolence? Much of the evaluation in church circles has been based on this statistical dimension. Most of the parochial reports are filled with statistical details and many of the reports at annual meetings of ecumenical agencies or of communions are filled with data. People call it "the numbers game." Committees looking for pastors or executives scan the records to see how the candidate fared in his present parish, or in previous parishes, and bishops or executives recommend for bet-

ter parishes those who have "produced the goods" statistically. Length is one dimension but it is only one!

2) *Breadth* is the second. How broad is the outreach?
How broad is the concern? The church of Jesus Christ
is a world-wide enterprise with concern for all people
of all ages and classes and cultures and clans. Church
programs that rate well statistically may fare less well
in this dimension, for the ministry may be limited to one
level, or to one section or to one class of people while
others are forgotten or ignored. Some may be deliberately left out because they are not the right kind of people.
The breadth dimension is concerned with the scope of
our ministry, and it needs to be faced. It raises the question as to where we serve, to whom, by whom, and with
what means. It asks whom are we neglecting and why.
And how can we reach and serve more widely than we
do? It is understood that a special program committee
or department may have a built-in limitation of scope
because it has an assigned task to do, like ministry to
agricultural migrants, or to a college campus, or to pre-
school children, or to handicapped. Even so the scope
question is valid, for within assigned areas these committees and boards still have broad range, and often
they narrow the field more than they should.

3) *Depth* is a third dimension. How deep does our
gospel witness go? How deep is the fellowship that we
experience and express in Christian congregations, or
in ecumenical relationships in which we profess to
believe? How deep is our service motivation? How deep
is our service? Even these preliminary questions make
people feel uneasy; yet they must be asked. Much of
the work of the churches does not penetrate beneath the
surface to challenge people to face up to the call of God's
spirit. We need to ask, "Do we witness to the grace and
truth of the gospel so that God's power can work through

that witness to change men and society?" Or is the accusation of the cynic fair when he claims that among his acquaintances there is really no difference between those who belong to the Christian church and those who do not belong? We have reason to wonder when in this land of more than 100,000,000 church members, our mental institutions are crowded, divorce and juvenile delinquency are on the increase, use of drugs is rampant, the crime rate soars, and corruption occurs in high places. Our Lord said "By their fruits ye shall know them." I am quite sure he was not referring to the statistical records of institutions. He saw fruits of his gospel in changed lives and in a changed society.

We need to ask also: "What is the depth of the fellowship in the Christian church?" In too many cases it is more like a service club than the body of Christ, and fellowship is identified as social and cultural affinity rather than the true reality of the church where "there is neither Jew nor Greek, there is neither bond nor free, there is neither male nor female, for ye are all one in Christ." Too often we identify a Christian service ministry with giving Thanksgiving baskets to needy families during the holiday season, and forget about the hungry during the other eleven months of the year. Service in depth is as much concerned about getting rid of slums as in coping with slum conditions. It plans and encourages wholesome youth activities as earnestly as it seeks to help delinquent youth. It gives food and shelter to the aged, but more than that it offers them worship and fellowship, and the social amenities of life as well. These are concerns at the depth dimension.

4) The final test, and the most penetrating of all, relates the Christian and the Christian churches directly to the Lord of the church in a vertical divine-human dimension. It tests our relationship to the Lord of the

church in terms of faithfulness and obedience. Instead
of asking questions or offering explanations, we need to
pause here for quiet prayer. Most of us do not find it
difficult to discover our failures at this point. We may
find it a little hard to confess them and to ask for pardon.
At the same time, we know deep down in our hearts
that faithfulness and obedience are the ultimate tests of
discipleship for Christians and for Christian churches.
At this vertical dimension we ask "What do you want
me to do Lord?" And when we hear the answer we
reply "Here am I, send me!" This may call for a solemn
Gethsemane—even Calvary! That was the way of the
master! Faced with this vertical dimension we say as
he said: "Nevertheless, not my will but thine be done."
It is quite possible that the church statistical record the
next month might have looked better if his answer had
been different. The same may be true for us. Yet the work
of the church of Jesus Christ requires obedience even
as our Lord was obedient, even unto death!

It is quite apparent that one can never get an adequate answer to the question of effectiveness by measur-
ing the church's work in only one dimension. We need
all four and we have suggested a fourfold approach as
a helpful basis for evaluation.

Model A and Model B can be related to each other;
they are not mutually exclusive. The reader may want
to develop a system of his own. The purpose of this
chapter is not to impose a system; it is rather to emphasize the importance and the propriety of evaluation as
a part of the leadership role in building the church of
Jesus Christ and in carrying forward its mission in the
world. We do not have the perfect system today; we will
not have the perfect system tomorrow. If we look critically at what we are doing today we may find better
means for doing God's work and accomplishing his will
in the tomorrows that are to come.

May the Lord bless us as we discover his church, as we find our place in it, and as we discover its mission in the community of time and place. May he bless us as we plan for this ministry, as we administer it, and as we evaluate our labors in his behalf, seeking to do his will as members of his church in our world!

Unity Confirmed by Communions

*Official statements
of church bodies
concerning Christian Unity*

CHURCH OF CHRIST UNITING (COCU)

The Church in Human Perspective

The church believes itself to be empowered for its task by the Spirit of God, who guides the community of faith in Christ's way and supplies the variety of gifts that are required for its common life.

But the church, in its humanness, falls short of its heritage and its destiny. The history of the church in every age reveals a duality in its life. The church is divine and human, holy and sinful, faithful and unfaithful.

The church is a community of those men and women of all ages and all places, of all races and tribes, who have been reconciled to God in Jesus Christ, who have received the Gospel of his redeeming love, who have been sealed and enabled by the Holy Spirit and who respond in faith, celebration, and obedient witness. It is a community bound in its life by the covenant of God with Israel which was made new in the life, death, and resurrection of Jesus Christ and will be consummated in the coming again of our Lord. It is bound together by a piomise and a hope. It understands its charge as that of constantly bearing witness to what it has heard and seen —through preaching and teaching the Word, through its celebration of the sacraments of baptism and the Lord's Supper, and through the faithful obedience of its life. It knows itself to be called into being by Christ the Son, who was sent into the world to show the Father's forgiving and redeeming grace for all mankind.[1]

On the pages that follow the church is described in biblical perspective much as described in Chapter 1 of this book. In theological perspective the COCU document emphasizes "truly catholic, truly evangelical, truly reformed," in line with Dr. Carson Blake's statement in his sermon at the Episcopal Cathedral in San Francisco in 1960, when the COCU proposal was first made.

CHURCHES IN COCU

United Methodist

A section of the constitution of the United Methodist Church, paragraph V, recorded in the Book of Discipline under date of 1968, reads:

Ecumenical Relations—As part of the Church Universal, The United Methodist Church believes that the Lord of the Church is calling Christians everywhere to strive toward unity, and therefore it will seek and work for unity at all levels of the church life: through world relationships with other Methodist churches and united churches related to The Methodist Church or The Evangelical United Brethren Church, through councils of churches, and through plans of union with churches of Methodist or other denominational traditions.

Episcopal

The text of the general convention report of the Episcopal Church meeting in Seattle, Washington, 1967, states the position of that church:

Whereas, This Church has, in the statement of the House of Bishops in Chicago, 1886, and in subsequent affirmations thereof, expressed its commitment to Church unity in the following terms:

1) Our earnest desire is that the Saviour's prayer 'that they may be one,' may, in its deepest and truest sense, be speedily fulfilled;

2) That we believe that all who have been duly baptized with water in the Name of the Father, and of the Son, and of the Holy Ghost, are members of the Holy Catholic Church;

3) That in all things of human ordering or human choice, relating to modes of worship and discipline, or to traditional customs, this Church is ready in the spirit of love and humility to forego all preferences of her own;

4) That this Church does not seek to absorb other communions, but rather, cooperating with them on the basis of a common Faith and Order, to discountenance schism, to heal the wounds of the Body of Christ, and to promote the charity which is the chief of Christian graces and the visible manifestations of Christ to the world; and

Whereas, The Consultation on Church Union, in *Principles of Church Union,* adopted in 1966, has declared: 'The people of God exist as one people, and only one, of every nationality and race and tongue. They have been made so in Christ; and He wills that they make this unity evident;' and, in its Open Letter to the Churches, has said: We recognize also that the united body proposed will still be far from the wholesome of the Body of Christ . . . . We have imagined this structure as best we could, to keep it open to all others who with ourselves seek a wider unity of Catholic and Evangelical tradition, alike reformed by every true obedience to God; now, therefore, be it

Resolved—that this General Convention affirm that the object of this Church's ecumenical policy is to press toward the visible unity of the whole Christian fellowship in the faith and truth of Jesus Christ developing and sharing in its various dialogues and consultations in such a way that the goal be neither obscured nor compromised and that each separate activity be a step toward the fulness of unity for which our Saviour prayed.

Presbyterian, U.S.

A statement prepared by the theological committee of the Presbyterian Church, U.S., and approved by the General Assembly of that church in 1964 contains an analysis of earlier documents with generous references to the *Ordinances* of John Calvin, and frequent quotations from statements of the World Council of Churches. It outlines four levels of interchurch relationship: Cooperation, Conciliar, Mutual Recognition, and Merger or Church Union. The document was prepared with concern for union and it sets forth three major guidelines for church union. These were: 1) faithful to the true ecumenical doctrine of the church; 2) preserve the essentials of the Christian gospel; and 3) deepen the spiritual life of the work of the church of Christ in the whole world.

The United Presbyterian in the U.S.A.

The United Presbyterian Church in the U.S.A. states in its constitution:

> The universal Church consists of all those persons, in every nation, together with their children, who make profession of the holy religion of Christ and of submission to his laws. (Chapter III, 33.02)
>
> Communions and particular churches ought to cooperate in so far as possible in giving expression to their oneness in Jesus Christ within His body, the ecumenical, Catholic Church. (Chapter III, 33.05)
>
> Particular churches of this Church may unite to form union churches with one or more particular churches of the Presbyterian Church in the United States, of the Reformed Church in America, and of other Reformed bodies, with the approval of the presbytery. (Chapter XXXVI, 66.01)

Particular churches of this Church may unite to form union churches with particular churches of other Churches, one or more of which are other than Churches with which General Assembly is in correspondence, with the approval of the presbytery and the General Assembly, provided that a Plan of Union, including the provisions set out in Sections 3 and 4 above, is adopted by the union church so formed. (Chapter XXXVI, 66.05)

The United Presbyterian Church in the U.S.A. has a Commission on Ecumenical Mission and Relations (COEMAR) which is described by the church as follows: (General Assembly, 1967)

Purpose: The Commission on Ecumenical Mission and Relations is an agency of the United Presbyterian Church which, as a member of the one Holy Catholic Church, is empowered by the Holy Spirit to go into the world:

—to make Jesus Christ known to all men as fellow man and divine Lord and Savior;

—to enter into the common life of men, sharing their aspirations and sufferings, striving against inhumanity, and healing the enmities which separate them from God and from each other;

—to encourage all men to become Christ's disciples and responsible members of His Church.

In service of this purpose, the Commission

—releases the resources of the United Presbyterian Church for the mission of the Church ecumenical outside the U.S.A.;

—explores and puts into action with other churches and ecumenical agencies wherever possible the forms our unity in the Spirit should take in our ministries;

—seeks on behalf of the United Presbyterian Church responsible participation in interchurch, confessional, and ecumenical organizations.

LUTHERAN CHURCHES

American Lutheran Church

In addition to its *Una Sancta* cantata, The American Lutheran Church established "guidelines for interchurch cooperation" which were approved at its 1968 convention. In these guidelines The American Lutheran Church affirms:

1. Our obligation to recognize that God is at work in and through other Christian churches.
2. Our obligation to determine the extent of our agreement with other churches in our understanding and interpretation of the Gospel, particularly in its application to contemporary life.
3. Our obligation to help one another as churches to make a united witness in proclaiming the Gospel of Jesus Christ to all men and nations.
4. Our obligation to cooperate with the Christian churches in works of love, in order to manifest the concern of God and of his people for the welfare of all men, such as the relief and eradication of human misery and injustice, the search for world peace, and the establishment of the rule of law in international affairs.

Then follows five principles of cooperation:

1. Our adherence to the evangelical principle whereby we recognize no other way of salvation than the way provided by the Triune God for the redemption of all mankind, accomplished through Jesus Christ in his death and resurrection, and conveyed by the Spirit of God in and through the Gospel in Word and Sacrament.
2. Our adherence to the biblical principle whereby the authority of the prophetic and apostolic Scriptures of the Old and New Testaments is established as the only rule and standard by which all doctrines and teachers must be judged.
3. Our adherence to the ecclesiastical principle whereby we affirm our faith in the 'one, holy, catholic,

[2][2][2][2][2][2][2][2][2][2][2][2][2][2][2][2][2][2][2][2][2][2][2][2][2][2][2][2][2][2][2][2][2][2][2][2][2][2][2][2][2][2][2][2][2][2][2][2][2][2][2][2][2][2][2][2][2][2][2][2][2][2][2][2][2][2][2][2][2][2][2][2][2][2][2][2][2][2][2][2][2][2][2][2][2][2][2][2][2][2]

and apostolic church'; and our reliance upon the Spirit of God to preserve us from error, compromise, or rejection of the truth of the Gospel.

4. Our adherence to the organizational principle whereby loyalty to the Lord and the Gospel according to the Scriptures always provides freedom to seek such forms of structure and common action in which Christian faith will find its most faithful witness, Christian love its most effective operation, and Christian hope its highest fulfillment.

5. Our adherence to the representational principle whereby in interchurch associations the official representatives of churches should never be expected to sit on a parity with individuals who represent only themselves or at most organizations which are less than churches.

Lutheran Church in America

Article IV of the Constitution of the Lutheran Church in America describes the nature of the Church as follows:

Section I.   All Power in the Church Belongs to our Lord Jesus Christ, its Head. All actions of this church are to be carried out under His rule and authority.

Section II.   The church exists both as an inclusive fellowship and as local congregations gathered for worship in Christian service. Congregations find their fulfillment in the universal community of the church, and the universal church exists in and through congregations. This church, therefore, derives its character and powers both from the sanction and representation of its congregations, and from its inherent nature as an expression of the broader fellowship of the faithful. In length, it acknowledges itself to be in the historic continuity of the Communion of Saints; in breadth it expresses the fellowship of believers in congregations in this, our day.

Article V of the LCA Constitution is more institutionally-oriented, but it gives specific directions:

to participate in ecumenical Christian activities, contributing its witness and work and cooperating with other churches which confess God, the Father, Son and Holy Ghost (Section 1-f).

to enter into relations with other Lutheran Church bodies and with other evangelical churches for the furtherance of the gospel of Our Lord (Section 1-m).

In its *Manifesto,* published in 1967, the Lutheran Church in America outlined a series of directives for action with clear ecumenical emphasis in relation to congregations. Five are pertinent in this context: "The Lutheran Church in America calls upon its congregations:

1. To support in prayer and to uphold in proclamation the oneness of the Church in all plans and at all times.
2. To recognize that it shares in the oneness of the Church through its reunion with other congregations in the Lutheran Church in America.
3. To see in its own life the presence of the Lutheran Church in America and in what this church does corporately in America and throughout the world an extension of its own mission, assuming a full and generous share of the responsibility which this entails.
4. To join with other Lutheran congregations, especially those nearby in mutual counsel and action gladly extending the fellowship of its pulpit and altar to all of them.
5. To engage in cooperative action with neighboring congregations and Councils of Churches which with it confess Jesus Christ as Lord and Saviour.[4]

Lutheran Church—Missouri Synod

In the *Mission Affirmations* approved by the Missouri Synod in 1965 the Church said under the general title *The Church Is Christ's Mission to the Church:*

Resolved—That we affirm as Lutheran Christians that the Evangelical Lutheran Church is chiefly a confessional movement within the total Body of Christ rather than a denomination emphasizing institutional barriers of separation. A Lutheran Christian uses the Lutheran confessions for the primary purpose for which they were framed: To confess Christ and His Gospel boldly and lovingly to all Christians. While the confessions seek to repel all attacks against the Gospel, they are not intended to be a kind of Berlin Wall to stop communication with other Christians, and be it further

Resolved—That we affirm that by virtue of our unity with other Christians in the Body of Christ we should work together when it will edify Christ's Body and advance His mission, refusing cooperation, however, on such occasions when it would deny God's word: . . .[5]

The *Report of the Commission on Theology and Church Relations* to the 1967 convention under the heading, "Fellowship with all Believers in Christ," affirms

Those who have fellowship with God through faith in Christ are also in fellowship with one another (1 John 1:3). As faith makes all men children of God, so it also makes them all brethren in Christ (Gal. 3:26 and 27). This fellowship transcends every barrier created by God or set up by man and brings about the highest unity possible among men, the unity in Christ Jesus (Gal. 3:28). This transcending of all barriers is beautifully described in Eph. 2:11-22.[6]

The *Report on Theology and Fellowship* concludes,

May our Lord Jesus Christ, who loved the church, and gave Himself for it (Eph. 5:25), protect and bless His church in all the world; may He Himself guide His children everywhere into all truth, and cleanse the church of all heresy and schism. May He bless also the church as it exists in The Lutheran Church—Missouri Synod and in the synods in fellowship with it. May He grant us grace to proclaim His Word with boldness and with power and to exhort with all longsuffering and doctrine (2 Tim. 4:2); to love the brotherhood (1 Peter 2:17); to speak the truth in love (Eph. 4:15); to walk worthy of the vocation wherewith we have been called, with all lowliness and meekness, with longsuffering, forbearing one another in love; endeavoring to keep the unity of the Spirit in the bond of peace, for there is one body and one Spirit, even as we are called in one hope of our calling; one Lord, one faith, one baptism, one God and Father of all, who is above all, and through all, and in us all (Eph. 4:1-6).[7]

Between these two clear and excellent unity statements are 21 pages of historical and analytical discussions and scriptural explanations which suggest a less generous approach of the Lutheran Church-Missouri Synod regarding church relations, and, in turn, explain the synod's aloofness from the total American church scene. However, the Lutheran Church-Missouri Synod with its strong emphasis on the Scripture and on creeds clearly affirms that there is only one church of Jesus Christ in all the world.

OTHER PROTESTANT CHURCHES

Reformed Church in America

An official statement of the Reformed Church in America, adopted in 1966 and re-affirmed in 1969, reads:

> The Reformed Church in America believes God calls forth through His Word and Holy Spirit from among lost men a people—His Church—whom He commissions to proclaim to the world His Gospel of Christ's redemption.
>
> This calling and commissioning belong to one Church, a uniting fellowship, having one Lord, one faith, one Baptism, one God and Father, and commissioned with one task to the one human race.
>
> We believe our task to be the proclamation of the Gospel of Jesus Christ as we worship the Lord when we hear His Word and celebrate the sacraments, as we witness the mighty acts of God in history, and we serve the world with a ministry of love.

In obedience to this divine revelation we of the Reformed Church in America resolve to manifest the God-given unity of the church by working to overcome our divisions. The ways and means to unity are not always known. The goal of Unity is a venture of faith. Therefore, trusting in the Holy Spirit for guidance we shall be open to His counsel, willing to converse with any church, ready to cooperate with all Christians, committed to participate in councils of churches on all levels, prepared to merge with any church when it is clearly the will of God, eager to heal the brokenness of the body of Christ in all ways known to us, until all are one, so that the world may know that the Father has sent the Son as Saviour and Lord.[8]

American Baptist Church

At its 1967 Convention the American Baptists made a statement on Christian unity which concludes with the following significant paragraphs:

Our basic concern is to achieve a continuous exploration of the possibility of Christian unity in all its manifestations and among all Christians everywhere. To do this, we must be willing to re-examine our basic traditions and practices in the light of Scripture, history, and our contemporary situation. We must be prepared to ask of ourselves, and of others, what is of first importance in the achievement of God's will for our time.

In our quest, we must ever bear in mind the purpose of Christ's coming in the first place—that mankind may know and experience the redemptive love of God that is able to transform our warring and broken world into a new humanity bound together in Christian love. Unity, then, in any of its manifestations, is not an end in itself, but a means whereby the ultimate mission of God's redemption of the world may be accomplished. We are called to nothing less than a most earnest response to what we believe is the summons of Jesus Christ, the Head of the church, to unity, renewal, and mission to the world.[9]

Southern Baptist Convention

The following statement, Article XIV of *The Baptist Faith and Message,* was adopted by the Southern Baptist Convention in 1963:

> Christ's people should, as occasion requires, organize such associations and conventions as may best secure cooperation for the great objects of the Kingdom of God. Such organizations have no authority over one another or over the churches. They are voluntary and advisory bodies designed to elicit, combine, and direct the energies of our people in the most effective manner. Members of the New Testament churches should cooperate with one another in carrying forward the missionary, educational, and benevolent ministries for the extension of Christ's Kingdom. Christian unity in the New Testament sense is spiritual harmony and voluntary cooperation for common ends by various groups of Christ's people. Cooperation is desirable between the various Christian denominations, when the end to be attained is itself justified, and when such cooperation involves no violation of conscience or compromise of loyalty to Christ and His Word as revealed in the New Testament.

ORTHODOX CHURCHES

A statement concerning the position of the Orthodox churches was prepared and presented to the Conference on Faith and Order, at Oberlin, and this statement appears in its entirety in Dr. Paul S. Minear's report of that conference. Two paragraphs from that statement set forth the position of Orthodox churches:

> If it be true that Christ founded the Church as a means of unifying men divided by sin, then it must naturally follow that the unity of the Church was preserved by his divine omnipotence. Unity, therefore, is not just a promise, or a potentiality, but belongs to the very nature of the Church. It is not something which has been lost and which should be recovered, but rather it is a permanent character of the structure of the Church.

Christian love impels us to speak candidly of our conviction that the Orthodox Church has not lost the unity of the Church intended by Christ, for she represents the oneness which in Western Christendom has only been a potentiality. The Orthodox Church teaches that she has no need to search for a "lost unity," because her historic consciousness dictates that she is the Una Sancta and that all Christian groups outside the Orthodox Church can recover their unity only by entering into the bosom of that Church which preserved its identity with early Christianity." [10]

Does the Orthodox statement sound a note of discord? The first paragraph quoted affirms the unity principle in ringing tones. Admittedly, the second paragraph comes as a shock to those who assume that visible unity will be achieved by some kind of fusion of many different parts into something quite new. The Orthodox church sees itself as carrying the continuing central core of the church within herself, and therefore understands visible unity as being achieved by returning to that core. This is made clear in a later paragraph of the same statement:

We are bound in conscience to state explicitly what is logically inferred; that all other bodies have been directly or indirectly separated from the Orthodox Church. The Unity from the Orthodox standpoint means a return of the separated bodies to the historical Orthodox, One, Holy, Catholic and Apostolic Church.[11]

ROMAN CATHOLIC CHURCH

Scriptures and the historic creeds are basic to doctrine in the Roman Catholic church as they are in other churches. On this basis the Roman Catholic church has affirmed the unity of the church from the beginning. Over many centuries of history, however, the Roman church has taken a hard line, almost sectarian position, ruling out the recognition of any but Roman Catholics as Christians.

The change since Vatican II has been remarkable. Since 1966 Living Room Dialogues between Roman Catholics and other Christians have taken place in hundreds of communities and Week of Prayer for Christian Unity celebrations have developed with significant Roman Catholic initiative. These activities bring Christians of many different traditions together in many ways. Furthermore, Reformation Day observances are becoming festivals of faith with full Roman Catholic participation.

These changes are related to the decisions and the expressions that came from the recent Vatican II Ecumenical Council. Its statements on the church and particularly its Decree on Ecumenism were most significant. The introduction to the decree on ecumenism reads:

> Promoting the restoration of unity among all Christians is one of the chief concerns of the Second Sacred Ecumenical Synod of the Vatican. The Church established by Christ is, indeed, one and unique. Yet many Christian communions present themselves to men as the true heritage of Jesus Christ. To be sure, all proclaim themselves to be disciples of the Lord, but their convictions clash and their paths diverge, as though Christ Himself were divided (cf. 1 Cor. 1:13). Without doubt, this discord openly contradicts and inflicts damage on the most holy cause of proclaiming the good news to every creature.

> Nevertheless, the Lord of Ages wisely and patiently follows out the plan of His grace on behalf of us sinners. In recent times He has begun to bestow more generously upon divided Christians remorse over their division and a longing for unity,

> Everywhere, large numbers have felt the impulse of this grace, and among our separated brethren also there increases from day to day a movement, fostered by the grace of the Holy Spirit, for the restoration of unity among all Christians. Taking part in this movement, which is called ecumenical, are those who invoke the Triune God and confess Jesus as Lord and Savior.[12]

Three pages later in that same decree we read:

> Moreover some, even very many, of the most significant elements or endowments which together go to build up and give life to the Church herself can exist outside the visible boundaries of the Catholic Church: the written word of God; the life of grace; faith, hope, and charity, along with other interior gifts of the Holy Spirit and visible elements. All of these, which come from Christ and lead back to Him, belong by right to the one Church of Christ.

> The brethren divided from us also carry out many of the sacred actions of the Christian religion. Undoubtedly, in ways that vary according to the condition of each Church or Community, these actions can truly engender a life of grace, and can be rightly described as capable of providing access in the community of salvation.

> It follows that these separated Churches and Communities, though we believe they suffer from defects already mentioned, have by no means been deprived of significance and importance in the mystery of salvation. For the Spirit of Christ has not refrained from using them as means of salvation which derive their efficacy from the very fullness of grace and truth entrusted to the Catholic Church.

> Nevertheless, our separated brethren, whether considered as individuals or as Communities and Churches, are not blessed with that unity which Jesus Christ wished to bestow on all those whom He has regenerated and vivified into one Body and newness of life—that unity which the holy Scriptures and the revered tradition of the Church proclaim. For it is through Christ's Catholic Church alone, which is the all-embracing means of salvation, that the fullness of the means of salvation can be obtained. It was to the apostolic college alone, of which Peter is the head, that we believe our Lord entrusted all the blessings of the New Covenant, in order to establish on earth the one Body of Christ into which all those should be fully incorporated who already belong in any way to God's People.[13]

The last two sentences of the above quotation indicate a position on the part of the Roman Catholic church similar to the Orthodox except that the core in this statement is the Roman Catholic church rather than the Orthodox church.

Even though the position is unacceptable to many, the tone of the decree on ecumenism is warm and conciliating, and Christians should rejoice in it. The unity of the church is affirmed. Non-Catholics are identified as "our separated brethren." They are acknowledged as brothers in the faith, with whom the Holy Spirit also works.

Chapter 3 of the decree concludes with an impressive paragraph on cooperation among Christian churches:

> Cooperation among all Christians vividly expresses that bond which already unites them, and it sets in clearer relief the features of Christ the Servant. Such cooperation, which has already begun in many countries, should be ever increasingly developed, particularly in regions where a social and technical evolution is taking place. It should contribute to a just appreciation of the dignity of the human person, the promotion of the blessings of peace, the application of gospel principles to social life, and the advancement of the arts and sciences in a Christian spirit. Christians should also work together in the use of every possible means to relieve the afflictions of our times, such as famine and natural disasters, illiteracy and poverty, lack of housing, and the unequal distribution of wealth. Through such cooperation, all believers in Christ are able to learn easily how they can understand each other better and esteem each other more, and how the road to the unity of Christians may be made smooth.[14]

There are parallels between the positions of the Orthodox and the Roman Catholic churches. Both affirm the basic unity of the church; both are interested in visible unity; both see real unity resulting as the divided churches return to their basic root; each claims to be the basic root.

While each of these churches claim to be the core to which the separated brethren should return for full realization of unity this position does not shut off dialogue between them and other Christians. In fact they now seem to welcome it to help clarify the areas of unity and of differences, and to learn from as well as to bear witness to, these separated brethren. Nor does the lack of full expression of visible unity hinder these churches from working with those churches with whom they differ in practical expression of common interest and concern and in common testimony concerning the unity thus far achieved.

Notes

Chapter 1   One Church

1. William Cate, *Ecumenical Scandal on Main Street* (New York: Association Press, 1965).

2. Paul Minear, *Nature of the Unity We Seek* (St. Louis: Bethany Press, 1958), pp. 122-124.

3. Paul J. Christiansen, *Una Sancta* (Minneapolis: Augsburg Publishing House, 1960).

4. Minear, pp. 28-29.

5. W. A. Visser 't Hooft, *New Delhi Speaks* (New York: Association Press, 1962), pp. 92-93.

6. *Yearbook of American Churches* (New York: National Council of Churches of Christ in the U.S.A., Department of Publication, 1970), pp. 110-115.

Chapter 2   One Mission

1. Forrest Knapp, *Church Cooperation: Dead End Street or Highway to Unity* (Garden City: Doubleday, 1966), p. 239.

Chapter 3   Mission in Community

1. M. R. Stein, *Eclipse of Community: An Interpretation of American Studies* (New York: Harper and Row).

Chapter 4   Community, U.S.A.

1. *Christ for the Moving Millions,* National Lutheran Council, 1955.

2. A standard metropolitan statistical area is defined by the Census Bureau as a central city of 50,000 population or more, plus the county or counties in which that city is located, and closely related counties.

Chapter 5   Planning for Mission in Community

1. If the planning concern is for an individual congregation the questions about the church may be worded differently, but the

same questions need to be asked. In congregational planning the questions about people should be asked about the church members as well as about the people in the neighborhood community. The information about people in the congregation can then be compared with the same information about people in the neighborhood. In many cases, this kind of simple comparison indicates areas of mission neglect, or areas of mission opportunity on the church's doorstep.

2. H. Richard Niebuhr, *Christ and Culture* (New York: Harper and Row, 1951).

Appendix: Unity Confirmed by Communions

1. *A Plan of Union*, COCU Distribution Center, Princeton, N.J., 1970, p. 15
2. *Ecumenical Actions of the General Convention of the Episcopal Church*, General Council, Protestant Episcopal Church, New York, 1967.
3. "American Lutheran Church and Interchurch Cooperation," Minneapolis, 1969, pp. 7-8.
4. Donald R. Pichaske, *The Manifesto* (Philadelphia: Fortress Press, 1967).
5. *Mission Affirmations*, Lutheran Church—Missouri Synod, 1965, Section III.
6. Report of the Commission on Theology and Church Relations, June, 1967, p. 7.
7. *Ibid.*, p. 28.
8. Report of General Synod, Acts and Proceedings, Reformed Church in America, New York, 1969, p. 290.
9. *Proceedings*, American Baptist Convention, Valley Forge, Pa., 1967.
10. Paul Minear, *Nature of the Unity We Seek*, pp. 160-161.
11. *Ibid.*, p. 161.
12. Walter M. Abbott, S.J., *Documents of Vatican II* (New York: Association Press, 1966), pp. 341-342.
13. *Ibid.*, pp. 345-346.
14. *Ibid.*, pp. 354-355.
15. Article XIV of *The Baptist Faith and Message*, Southern Baptist Convention, Nashville, Tenn., 1963.

Bibliography

Chapter 1 — *ONE CHURCH*

Abbott, Walter M. *Documents of Vatican II,* Association Press, 1966.

Aulen, Gustav. *Faith of the Christian Church,* Fortress Press, 1961.

Bea, Augustin Cardinal. *The Unity of Christians,* Herder and Herder, 1963.

Cate, William. *Ecumenical Scandal on Main Street,* Association Press, 1965. o.p.

Cavert, Samuel. *Church Cooperation and Unity in America 1900-1970,* Association Press, 1970.

Cavert, Samuel. *The American Churches in the Ecumenical Movement, 1900-1968,* Association Press, 1968.

Day, Peter. *Tomorrow's Church: Catholic, Evangelical, Reformed,* Seabury Press, 1969.

Flew, R. Newton. *Nature of the Church,* Harper and Row, 1952. o.p.

Knapp, Forrest. *Church Cooperation: Dead End Street or Highway to Unity,* Doubleday, 1966. o.p.

Küng, Hans. *The Church,* Sheed and Ward, 1968.

McBrien, Richard P. *Do We Need the Church?,* Harper and Row, 1969.

Minear, Paul. *Images of the Church in the New Testament,* Westminster Press, 1960.

Sanderson, Ross. *Church Cooperation in the United States,* Findlay, 1960.

Welch, Claude. *Reality of the Church,* Charles Scribners Sons, 1958.

Williams, Colin. *New Directions in Theology Today,* Vol. 4 "The Church." Westminster Press, 1965.

Chapter 2 — *ONE MISSION*

Berger, Peter. *Noise of Solemn Assemblies,* Doubleday, 1961.

Niebuhr, H. Richard. *The Purpose of the Church and Its Ministry,* Harper and Row, 1956.

Ranck, J. Allen. *Education for Mission,* Friendship Press, 1961.

Chapter 3 — *MISSION IN COMMUNITY*

Gottmann, Jean. *Megalopolis,* 20th Century Fund, 1961.

Huff and Kelly. *Ecumenical Designs,* Church and Community Life, 1969.

Lee, Robert. *Cities and Churches,* Westminster Press, 1962.

Moore, Paul. *The Church Reclaims the City,* Seabury Press, 1964. o.p.

Stein, Maurice. *Eclipse of Community,* Harper and Row, 1966.

Weber, George. *God's Colony in Man's World,* Abingdon, 1960.

Williams, Colin. *What in the World,* Department of Publications, NCC, 1964.

Chapter 5 —
PLANNING FOR MISSION IN COMMUNITY

Duncan, Otis Dudley. *Metropolis and Region,* John Hopkins, 1960. o.p.

Goodenough, Ward. *Cooperation in Change,* Russell Sage, 1963.

Warren, E. Kirby. *Long Range Planning,* Prentice Hall, 1966.

Kloetzle and Hillman. *Urban Church Planning,* Fortress, 1958.

Niebuhr, H. Richard. *Christ and Culture,* Harpers, 1951.

Norton, Perry. *Search,* National Council of Churches, 1960.

Schaller, Lyle. *Planning for Protestantism in Urban America,* Abingdon, 1965.

Schen, Donald. *Theology and Change,* Delacorte Press, 1967. o.p.

Wieser, Thomas. *Planning for Mission,* U.S. Conference of WCC, 1966.

Chapter 6 — *FROM PLAN TO ACTION*

Drukher, Peter. *The Practice of Management,* Harper and Row, 1954.

Etzioni, Amitai. *Modern Organizations,* Prentice-Hall, 1964.

Gardner, John. *Self Renewal,* Harper and Row, 1964.

Flory, Charles, ed. *Managers for Tomorrow,* New American Library (Revised) 1965.

Judy, Marvin T. *The Multiple Staff Ministry,* Abingdon, 1969.

Levitt, Theodore. *Innovation in Marketing,* McGraw-Hill, 1962.

Lyden and Miller, eds. *Planning—Programming—Budgeting: A Systems Approach to Management,* Markham, 1967.

Thompson, T. K. *Handbook of Stewardship Procedures,* Prentice-Hall, 1965. o.p